FOOD AND LOVE

the

amazing

connection

between . . .

food&

&love

FOREWORD BY
REX RUSSELL, M.D.

DR. GARY
SMALLEY

TYNDALE HOUSE PUBLISHERS, INC., WHEATON, ILLINOIS

Visit Tyndale's exciting Web site at www.tyndale.com

Food and Love

Copyright © 2001 by Smalley Publishing Group, LLC. All rights reserved.

Cover art copyright © 2001 by Michael Hudson. All rights reserved.

Author photo copyright © 2001 by Jim Lersch. All rights reserved.

Published in association with the literary agency of Alive Communications, Inc., 7680 Goddard Street, Suite 200, Colorado Springs, CO 80920.

Designed by Dean H. Renninger

Edited by Lynn Vanderzalm

In sharing stories from other people's lives in this book, I have changed their names and some of the details of their stories in order to protect their privacy.

Unless otherwise indicated, all Scripture quotations are taken from the *Holy Bible,* New Living Translation, copyright © 1996. Used by permission of Tyndale House Publishers, Inc., Wheaton, Illinois 60189. All rights reserved.

Scripture quotations marked NIV are taken from the *Holy Bible,* New International Version®. NIV®. Copyright © 1973, 1978, 1984 by International Bible Society. Used by permission of Zondervan Publishing House. All rights reserved.

Scripture quotations marked NASB are taken from the *New American Standard Bible,* © 1960, 1962, 1963, 1968, 1971, 1972, 1973, 1975, 1977 by The Lockman Foundation. Used by permission.

Scripture marked The Message is taken from *The Message.* Copyright © by Eugene H. Peterson, 1993, 1994, 1995. Used by permission of NavPress Publishing Group. All rights reserved.

Library of Congress Cataloging-in-Publication Data

Smalley, Gary.
   Food and love : the amazing connection / Gary Smalley ; foreword by Rex Russell.
     p. cm.
   Includes bibliographical references.
   ISBN 0-8423-5520-0 (alk. paper) — ISBN 0-8423-5522-7 (pbk. : alk. paper)
   1. Food—Psychological aspects.   I. Title.
TX357 . S54 2001
641.3′01′9—dc21   2001003509

Printed in the United States of America

05 04 03 02 01
8   7   6   5   4   3   2   1

I dedicate this book to my eight precious grandchildren.
May they grow up better understanding how the foods they
eat affect the quality of their love and health.

Michael Thomas Gibson

Taylor Christine Smalley

Baby Roger Thomas Gibson

Cole Gregory Smalley

Hannah Elise Gibson

Madalyn Murphy Smalley

Reagan Elizabeth Smalley

Garrison Patrick Thomas Smalley

CONTENTS

I n my experience as a doctor, I've learned at least this: When problems are bigger than our collective brain trusts can solve, typically there's an answer in Scripture, and almost always it's an answer that's been staring us in the face since the beginning of time.

When Gary Smalley told me he was doing a book about the amazing connection between food and love and that he wanted to draw extensively on my research about biblical eating, I felt like shouting to the world: "Someone's finally getting it!"

The truth is this: God gave us a fantastic blueprint for what to eat and how to love. However, we need only look around us to see how people are failing in both areas. Recent medical statistics show that obesity is up from 12 percent of the population in 1991 to 20 percent in 1999. It's epidemic, and it's not only destroying our bodies, but as Gary will show you, our relationships as well.

It's about time we realized the connection.

What Gary has done here is pull together the very latest research to show a dynamic that has always existed between how we eat and how we love. Beyond that he's shown that how we love affects our health. In fact, how we love is even more of an influence than what we eat when it comes to our health. It's fantastic information, and I believe it could be life changing for an entire generation of Americans.

What I like best about this book is Gary's dedication to truth. Not only has he used research and personal experience to demonstrate the connection between food and love. But he's taken that research to the next level by explaining how—for many people—the cycle of poor eating and poor relating cannot be broken on their own strength.

But only by God's power.

Rest assured that I have verified the information regarding health and nutrition in this book and agree that it is consistent with the very latest research. However, before you change your personal diet or exercise plan, be sure to check with your doctor.

That said, I believe the answers to your eating and relating dilemmas could very well be just beyond the next page. Enjoy the journey!

REX RUSSELL, M.D.
AUTHOR OF *WHAT THE BIBLE SAYS ABOUT HEALTHY LIVING*

ACKNOWLEDGMENTS

he writing of a book is never the work of only one person. Many people have come together to make this significant book possible, and I owe them my deepest thanks.

I thank Karen Kingsbury, who helped me write the book. I found out about Karen's writing when a friend asked me to read one of her fiction books, *A Moment of Weakness*.

I read the book on a cross-country flight with my son Greg, and I guess my crying got a little too loud. Greg had to tap me on the shoulder and ask me to keep it down; I was embarrassing him. I love stories. I love to read quality books that make me laugh and cry and change the way I live. After reading Karen's book, I have to say that she is my favorite fiction author. I've now read everything she's written and truly believe that one day everyone will know about her books. All that to say, I couldn't have written this book without her help, and I thank God that she has agreed to work with me for years to come.

I also thank Greg Johnson, easily the best agent in the publishing industry, not only for having the amazing and creative ability to put together contracts that will glorify God but also for shepherding me through what feels like a second publishing life.

A special thanks goes to Dr. Rex Russell for agreeing to oversee the nutritional accuracy of the material for this book and for realizing what God is saying about healthy eating. Also thanks to the dozens of doctors and nutritionists whose books helped me realize a connection that changed my life.

I am also indebted to Steve McVey, whose books have had a profound impact on my thinking about the role of God's grace and power in the connection between food and love.

Thanks certainly goes to the Tyndale people who caught my vision for this book. Ken Petersen, Ron Beers, Lynn Vanderzalm, and everyone—from Sales to Marketing—I couldn't have done this book without you. I thank God for this new and wonderful relationship we share.

A heartfelt thanks goes to my sons, Greg and Mike, and the wonderful people at the Smalley Relationship Center. Your feedback has helped turn my random thoughts and dreams into a book I believe will help countless people across the country. Thanks to my daughter, Kari, and son-in-law, Roger, for your incredible insight. I love you all and treasure the role you play in my life each day.

Finally, a deep and abiding thanks to my wife, Norma, who has made it possible for me to achieve all of my greatest dreams. Through the decades of our marriage she has been a patient and gracious companion. While I was out training other people about how to have a better marriage and family, Norma supported me and made sure that our home was a stable and nurturing environment. She has always been the glue that held everything together at home and at work. I couldn't do what I do without her willingness to learn with me the ways to have a great relationship. I love you more than you know, Norma.

PART 1

WHY FOOD AND LOVE?

CHAPTER ONE

A Personal Journey

D id you know that certain foods could be harming your relationships? Have you ever considered that your relationships may be harming your health? Both are strong possibilities, and the connection between them is an area that is rarely talked about in relationship education.

Until now.

Through my own personal experience and years of reading and research, I have stumbled onto an amazing connection between two of the most powerful and passionate forces in our lives: eating and loving. In the process I finally understand what is perhaps the only way to make lasting change in either area.

It's the most exciting information I've come across in years.

Although many factors contribute to our emotional, relational, and physical health, very few professionals are commenting on the way eating and relating affect our overall well-being. In dealing with that issue personally, I recognized a connection I hadn't seen or heard discussed before.

Now I have no choice but to share that information with you. Why? Because I believe the material here could quite possibly help you find a new way of eating or a new way of relating. Maybe, like me, you'll lose weight in the process and feel better than ever about your ability to love.

The bottom line is this: If you're like me, the material in this book might give you the breakthrough you've been waiting for.

In the following pages I have the privilege of sharing with you the connection between food and love, and the way it changed my life. This is not a scientific book; rather it is a presentation of personal experiences—both in my own life and in the lives of thousands of people I've surveyed or counseled—along with current research on the topic of food and love.

The connection is this:

- Our food choices can affect our emotional health;
- Our emotional health definitely affects our relationships;
- Our relationships affect our physical and emotional health;
- Our emotional and physical health can affect our food choices.

Most of us know that food affects our *physical* health; we see that in the impact food has on conditions like heart disease, blood pressure problems, diabetes, and so many others. We already know that our relationships affect our *emotional* health; we see that in the impact fractured or unstable relationships have on our moods.

But what we haven't explored in detail is the connection between food and love, a connection that takes place when food affects our emotions, our emotions affect our relationships, and our relationships affect our health. That's the connection, the cycle, I want to share with you in this book. For most people this cycle is ongoing and will continue throughout life—positively or negatively.

We can picture the cycle like this (SEE FIGURE 1):

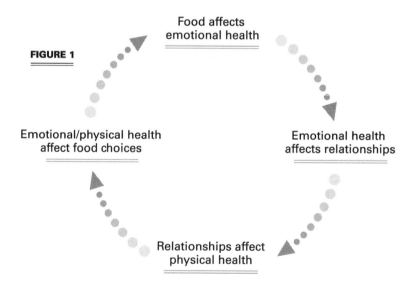

FIGURE 1

Food affects
emotional health

Emotional health
affects relationships

Relationships affect
physical health

Emotional/physical health
affect food choices

For most of my life, I have made poor food choices because I didn't know any better. I didn't have adequate information. But despite my poor eating habits, I never had much of a weight problem. Then several years ago

I got caught in the trap of overeating, and I became obsessive about foods—both wanting the wrong kinds and being upset with myself when I ate them.

This, then, affected my moods, making me a little more edgy and sluggish, and those moods strained most of my relationships. That, in turn, affected my physical health. This entire experience caused me stress, and in my attempts to deal with the stress, I ate even more.

I couldn't break the cycle until I recognized the connection and realized that change didn't seem to come through my own willpower. I knew I needed help from somewhere, but I couldn't find the way out of the cycle.

The heart of this book came when I realized that at some point in our lives most of us struggle with these two powerful forces: food and love. Most of us want to be as healthy as possible and to enjoy satisfying relationships. But the majority of us, when we're really honest, fall short in both areas.

We fall short for one of two reasons: Either we lack the knowledge to change, or we lack the willpower. If you struggle in the areas of food and love because you have never known the amazing connection between the two, then this book will give you significant information that could change your life. If you know what you need to do about food but you don't have the willpower to make the necessary changes, then part 6—Steps to Lasting Change—may help you find the strength you've never had before.

Before we get started, let me share with you how the information in this book changed my life.

WHEN I FELL IN LOVE WITH FOOD

As I was growing up, I could eat whatever I wanted and never gain a pound. I could have four sandwiches for lunch. I could eat all day long, and because of a combination of my metabolism and activity level, I burned it off. Weight was never a problem for me.

"Eating like that will catch up to you one day, Gary," friends would say. But it never did, and in my ignorance I thought it never would.

My father had died of a heart attack when he was fifty-eight years old, and my older brother had died of the same thing at age fifty-one. Another brother had undergone triple-bypass surgery. Obviously heart problems run in our family.

I was forty-seven when my older brother died. The relationship he and I shared had become very close, and his death was a terrible shock to my system. For a while I ate differently—less fat, that kind of thing—because I was concerned about my heart. But then I slipped back into my old ways. My arteries may have been developing serious problems, but I felt healthy and had no motivation to change.

Then I hit my fifty-eighth birthday.

Almost immediately my overeating began expanding my midsection. I would eat two breakfast meals, big lunches, two dinners. Overnight, it seemed, I fell in love with food. I had never loved it before, but I acquired new tastes for different kinds of food, foods that satisfied me in a deep way.

At the same time, circumstances in my career were subtly straining the relationship between my wife, Norma, and me. Looking back, I realize that I may have turned to food as a means of comfort because of that strain. In a sense, food became love for me, my way of feeling good and rewarding myself at the end of a long day.

I rationalized saying, "Oh, I'll be okay. Before long, I'll stop this pattern and start losing weight."

Instead, I kept gaining weight.

My love for food grew, and I began finding more pleasure in eating than ever before. It was as if my poor food choices had affected me emotionally, causing me to direct my feelings away from Norma and the people in my life, and more toward what I ate.

It was a very new experience.

I would hang out at dessert tables, eating until I was far too full, all because I enjoyed the taste and comfort the sweets provided. I found this principle at work: The more I ate, the more I wanted. When I woke up tired and bloated, heavier than the day before, I still wanted more. I craved doughy foods with fats and sugars, and I knew no way to control my appetite. At times I went to bed feeling uneasy and full of self-condemnation because of the things I was eating. But I knew no way to stop.

Without warning, I had the same problem that so many other people do, a problem I once ignorantly thought was easy to handle. But when the problem was mine, I saw the truth: I was completely helpless; there was nothing I could do about it.

A year of living like that humbled me in my attitude toward health and relationships like nothing else could have. I remembered the shameful way I had treated family members and friends who struggled with weight. I sadly admit that I had had very little patience with overweight people. I became frustrated with their lack of self-control. Inwardly I judged them as indulgent people, and I often tried to make them feel guilty, tried to be their conscience, and tried to monitor their food intake. I would keep a close eye on their serving sizes and cast them disgusted looks if they took a piece of dessert at a social gathering. Big mistake!

Back then I tried to make other people change their ways and lose a few pounds. But the truth was, all I ever did in the process was push them away from me, make them doubt my love, and drive them further into a lifestyle of finding comfort in food.

Once the weight problem was mine, I began to understand a connection between what I ate, how I felt about myself, and the way I treated those around me. I also realized that I was absolutely helpless over my increasing weight problem and declining health. I had neither the desire nor the willpower to stop eating the foods that were harming me. To my wife's credit, she was completely gracious to me, not treating me the way she saw me treat others.

As my battle with food and excess weight raged, it became a war, and I realized that in a few short years it would ultimately kill me. I prayed daily for an answer.

In what seemed like a coincidence at that time, I started reading books about living in God's strength, although I never thought the information I learned would relate to my food choices. The more I read and counseled others, the more I realized that the country is full of people like me—people struggling with eating right and loving right. Could their problems and mine be a result—at least in part—of the connection I was seeing? Could food truly play a part in harming a person's relationships? Could weak relationships really harm a person's physical health? And was it possible that a person's overall health might affect the way that person made food choices?

I believed I had stumbled onto something that might change my life, so I kept praying, researching, and believing God had something he was trying to show me.

RECOGNIZING GOD'S POWER

I continued studying about God's power, and one morning it was as if a lightbulb went off. I thought, Wait a minute! If God's power can help us in every area of our lives, every habit, then his power could save me from overeating. After all, it isn't his will that I overeat, but I can't control it anymore.

Without telling anyone, that October morning I decided I would try an experiment to see if God's strength could break my cycle of poor eating and poor relating. I had nothing to lose—except weight! I knew that I was out of options other than this last-ditch attempt: to give my struggle to God and seek his best for my life, through his strength alone.

So I got on my knees and cried out to God. I patterned my cry after the passage in Psalms, "Call upon me in the day of trouble; I will deliver you, and you will honor me."[1]

Still on my knees, I admitted that I could not control my eating, that I had tried, and that the task was beyond me. My own abilities were not sufficient. I came to God and said, "I can't seem to do this on my own. It's not going to happen through my own efforts."

I felt as if I were kneeling at the foot of the cross and asking God to free me. Since this was my own personal experiment, I had nothing to lose except my weight.

I had cried out to God this way before, but only about temporary issues or crises. Never had I figured out how desperately I needed God's power to find lifelong victory over an integral part of my life. I still didn't fully understand the connection between food and love. But from that moment on I relaxed and rested in God. I waited on him and said, "You can do this in me anytime you want." In the meantime, though, I knew I couldn't control my overeating.

This was where my waiting period started.

Since I didn't have power on my own to change my eating habits, what did I do? I kept eating. I never even tried to stop. Daily I said to God, *Father, however you want me to eat, I'm willing to do that. Whatever you want me to learn or do, just show me.* Sometimes I would ask, *Do you want me to read something or talk to someone or meet someone who has an answer for me? Anything you want me to do, just show me. I'll see it as a miracle and an act of your strength in my life.*

He began to make even clearer the definition of his strength in my life. God alone can give us the power to live life fully. That's really it in a few words. So I waited and rested, and rested and waited.

The days wore on, and I continued to say, *God, I'm still out of control here, and if you would heal me today, I would be more than grateful. But I'm just going to wait; I'm not going to chase after a bunch of how-to books or use my energy and efforts to do this on my own. I'm really going to see if this works in my life.*

I know what you're thinking.

The very volume you're holding is a how-to book. But there's a difference. When you wait on God's strength for victory, you won't have to chase after things to read; God will simply place them in your path. When he does, allow for the fact that a how-to book—perhaps even this one—could possibly provide the breakthrough you're looking for.

For me, the more I prayed, the more convinced I became that God would take care of my eating problem. Soon I wasn't telling God I wanted to see *if* his power worked in this area of my life. Rather I wanted to see *when* it would work. I grew more excited with each passing week.

During that waiting time I recalled other instances in which God's strength was all that pulled me through—even though I hadn't fully recognized the fact at the time. There were days when I would tell God, *You've worked powerfully in my life before, and I know you'll do it again. I just don't know how long it is going to take or how you are actually going to do it.*

I refused to give in to fear.

It's easy for us to worry, but that isn't how God wants us to live when we're in a relationship with him. I reminded myself that the Bible says, "Whatever is good and perfect comes to us from God above, who created all heaven's lights. Unlike them, he never changes or casts shifting shadows."[2] I told myself that God doesn't sit in heaven and say, "Let's see. How can I make life miserable for Gary Smalley?" In addition I was able to trust that all things work together for the good of those who love God and have been called according to his purpose.[3]

Basically I decided to be confident that God's will was better than mine. I would rather wait for his power than keep failing by relying on my own strength.

And so I waited.

STILL WAITING

October and November went by, and I kept overeating, kept gaining weight. But I had completely stopped worrying about it. I didn't feel guilty or condemned.

And yes, once in a while I had doubts.

Like every other American, I like things done instantly. As the days wore on, the doubts grew worse.

Looking back now, I know that God used that time to teach me empathy toward people who have difficulty with their weight. I can honestly say I understand those people so much better now. God helped me know how hurtful my thoughts and opinions had been, how judgmental and critical I had acted in the past.

Especially toward people I knew well and loved.

God used that time to teach me deep and significant truths, but back then the waiting was very difficult. Thanksgiving Day hit with all the big meals, all the pies, all the leftovers. I loved it and ate as much as I wanted—and then some. I'm sure I gained another twenty pounds that fall. I began to think, *Wow, I'm going to be as big as a house before long.* I couldn't see any end to my struggle.

Why? Because I loved food more than ever before. But still I kept waiting.

Finally, in mid-December, I was speaking at a university in California, where most of my relatives live. My niece Debbie Smalley was saying good-bye to me at the airport when she handed me a book. "I've been reading this, and it's been really helpful. It's the best book on food I've ever read. It was so motivating for me." (Was my eating really that obvious?)

I stood there dumbfounded. Debbie knew nothing of what I was doing. She didn't know I was praying that God would free me from my overeating problem and from what for me had become a food addiction. I still hadn't told anyone of my private experiment with letting go of my own abilities and letting God take over. Certainly my eating habits did not give clues that I was anxious to change.

I took the book and kept myself from looking surprised. But what I wanted to say was, "Debbie, I don't need a book on eating." At that moment, it never occurred to me that I had been praying for that very thing—some type of breakthrough given to me by God's design.

It fascinates me now as I look back because only God could have prompted her to give me that book. I put it in my briefcase and thanked her. I didn't think about it again until halfway through my flight. My speaking engagement that day had drained me, and I was flat-out exhausted. I planned to sleep the whole flight.

The last thing I wanted to do on that airplane was read a book. Especially a book about how to eat. I already knew how to do that. But partway into the flight, I had a strong impression that had to be from God: *Get that book out of your briefcase!*

I looked around and saw that no one was talking to me. *This is crazy!*

I thought. *I'm too tired to read. I would probably read two paragraphs and be sound asleep.*

But I took the book out.

I still didn't realize that God might be trying to get my attention with that particular book. He speaks to each of us differently, but at that moment in time he wanted me to read that book. Why? Because he alone knew what it would take to reach me.

The book *What the Bible Says about Healthy Living* is written by Dr. Rex Russell. My first thought was, *I don't even want to know this information.* Then I heard that still small voice rattling around in the basement of my heart again: *Read this book, will you! Are you not praying to me to free you? Read the book!*

I sighed out loud. "Okay, God, I'll read it."

THE MIRACLE

I figured I would pick up the book, glance at a few pages, and skim it for a few minutes. Maybe read it later. Instead I read the first page. Then the second and the third and the fourth. Minutes passed, and I could literally feel my eyes being opened for the first time. I could sense my spirit, my whole life opening up to facts about nutrition that I had been vaguely aware of but had never accepted.

It was the moment I had been praying for.

Let me say again that it wasn't the book that gave me the miracle I had been praying for. It was God. And in his grace he knew what it would take to give me the change I had been praying for. Many of you could read a book like this one and find it filled with material you have read a hundred times before. It might leave you totally unmoved.

The point isn't *how* God gives you a breakthrough; the point is that he *will*. God in his grace and strength will find a way to meet you where you are.

You see, I had slipped into a negative cycle regarding the connection between food and love. I made poor food choices, and those were harming my emotional health. At the same time, my poor emotional health was harming my relationship with close friends, loved ones, and others. That, in turn, was harming my physical health—contributing to my weakened immune system and high blood pressure.

I needed a miracle to break this cycle, and you may need a miracle, too.

God used Rex Russell's book to give me my breakthrough, but yours might be a conversation or an attitude adjustment or a magazine article or a sermon. Maybe you'll experience your breakthrough after reading the seven steps to lasting change in part 6 of this book. Only God knows.

Anyway, after reading the book, I felt released of the urge to overeat. I felt free and clean on the inside! I was excited and hopeful. Everything in the book made so much sense, I had to wonder where this information had been for fifty-eight years of my life.

Rex Russell's way of looking at food and how we eat opened my eyes to a whole new world of health. Some of what the book said was not new to me, but the way the information was put together was just right for me. I could feel God's power inside, allowing me to make a decision then and there. I didn't want to eat again, not until I finished the book, reread it, outlined it, and understood it. Not until I could start implementing the information in my own life. It was like a quiet power at work inside me.

From that moment on I felt total freedom, and that led to a four-day fast. I had no desire to eat! I had no hunger pains, and I wasn't light-headed. When I fasted in the past, I would feel weak and even faint when I would stand up. I had none of that. I was so charged up with God's strength that I was absolutely sure this was his answer to my prayers.

It was a total miracle for me.

Operating in God's strength, I read the information in the book, understood it, and instantly stopped my destructive eating habits. Later in this book I'll share some of Rex Russell's guidelines to healthy, biblical eating—not because it's the only way to eat, but because it helped me. Maybe it'll help you, too.

Healthy eating led to the next discovery—that with my new food choices, I recognized vast improvements in my emotional health. This in turn helped me love my family better, to be more empathetic and kind, more compassionate, and more the person they needed me to be. As this new dynamic took root in my life, my physical health improved. Finally, my improved health has helped me to continue making healthy food choices. And that's how I stumbled onto the amazing connection between food and love.

During this time I read dozens of books and found volumes of research that underscored the truths I was recognizing. Next, I interviewed thousands of people and found that they, too, had seen this cycle, this connection at work in their lives—negatively or positively. That information is included in this book as well.[4]

Today I am thrilled to tell you that nothing about food choices, my emotional health, my relationships, my physical health, or my spiritual health has been the same since. I not only lost all the extra weight by eating healthy food but also experienced many other unexpected benefits. I have been so healthy during the past few years that I have not had any illnesses, not even a cold. All of the joint and muscle soreness and stiffness that I experienced for years are gone, even after spending many hours doing rigorous manual labor. A truly miraculous consequence is that one day after I fell off my tractor and landed on my back, I had no pain or stiffness the next day—a remarkable thing for a person my age. I can only conclude that this newfound health is the result of my healthy eating habits. I lost all the extra weight by eating healthy food, a process I'll describe later.

One of the important outcomes of my battle with food is that God used it to convict me about how insensitive I had been to others in their struggles with food. When I look back on all of the years I hurt people with my rude comments, I see the grace they extended to me—grace I should have been giving them. I'm so grateful that they not only have forgiven me but also accepted me despite my insensitive behavior. I realize that I messed up in two very powerful ways. First, I tried to change them, which strained my relationship with them; and second, I refused to see how God wanted to change *me* and change the way I treated other people. In the process, I only made things worse—both for others and for myself.

I learned something very important about the connection between food and love in this process: *As important as eating correctly is for our health, having strong, loving relationships is even more important.* In fact, a loving relationship can almost overcome the damage of poor foods. But with my critical spirit toward those who were overweight, I weakened important relationships in my life, and in the process I weakened my own health.

As the result of my personal journey, I bring you this book.

No, it doesn't contain all the answers, and certainly it doesn't contain the definitive answers to a myriad of complex issues involving food, emotional health, relationships, and physical health. But it contains information that helped change my life and the lives of thousands of others, and it recognizes a connection that might help you find the breakthrough you're looking for. Perhaps as you read, you will see yourself, and in the process you, too, will find change.

CHAPTER TWO

The Amazing Connection

Barbara was in marriage counseling by the time she realized the connection between food and love. She came home from her first appointment with the counselor and found her husband, Jim, at the computer doing research.

For a moment she hesitated. He had rejected her so often in the past ten years that Barbara wasn't sure she could take any more. But the counselor had advised her to talk to Jim and open up lines of communication. Barbara knew there was no time like the present to start. She moved behind him and placed her hands on his shoulders. She bent her head near his and nuzzled against his cheek, saying, "Honey, I think I'm starting to learn how God wants us to treat each other."

Jim's shoulders tensed beneath her touch. Like an accident victim in a neck brace, he turned stiffly and stared at her. "Don't get religious on me just because you saw that marriage guy, okay?"

Barbara could feel the tears pricking at her eyes. She blinked. "I'm serious, Jim. This is something we need to talk about."

He sighed and turned all the way around, pushing his chair back to create distance between them. "Look, Barbara. The best thing you could do for our marriage is find a diet that works." He hesitated, and Barbara could tell by the shadow that fell over his face that he regretted his words. "What I mean is, you and I are just fine without God's help or anyone else's for that matter. I just think we would be better if, well, if . . . you know . . . if you lost some weight."

The hurt in Barbara's heart was sudden and crippling. She had to force herself not to drop in a heap at his feet. Instead, she nodded and quickly turned around, barely making it to the stairs before the sobs took over.

"Barbara?" he called after her. "Great, now I've done it. What's wrong? Come on, why do you always have to be so sensitive?"

Barbara ignored his questions. She made it to the bathroom, planted herself in front of the mirror, and gave in to a torrent of tears.

She recognized the fact that she had been overeating, binge eating even, for longer than she could remember. The excess food had caused her to gain weight, a problem that was harming her self-image and detracting seriously from her emotional health. This in turn caused her to withdraw from her husband, a subconscious move that then led to her feelings of isolation.

That day in counseling she realized for the first time that her isolation and distant relationship with her husband were very likely some of the factors contributing to her poor physical health. The end result was that whereas she once sought comfort and love from her husband, she was now finding those things from food.

It was a terrible cycle, and Barbara—like so many of us—had no idea how to change it.

As she looked in the mirror, she spoke to the woman who had almost become a stranger to her: "What . . . what happened to you? What did you do with Barbara?"

SEEING THE CONNECTION

Food and love.

All of it was intricately connected for Barbara, but at that point in her life she knew only that she was miserable. She was forty-two years old, nearly eighty pounds overweight, and suffering from hypertension, depression, and the early signs of heart disease and diabetes. Before Barbara had allowed food to rule her life, Jim used to come home, embrace her, give her a lingering kiss, and ask about her day. Now he stayed late at the office, and she couldn't remember the last time they had hugged.

The beautiful physical relationship the two of them had shared in their early years was nothing but a memory, and most days Barbara didn't want to live to see nightfall. Worst of all, every self-driven attempt she made at change in both her marriage and her health resulted in failure.

"I'm trapped in an unhappy marriage and a prison of unhealthy fat," she told the counselor on her next visit. "Diets fail me, health books fail me, now my marriage is failing, too. My husband thinks that it's my fault, that I'm not trying hard enough. Is there any way out?"

Barbara was like me and many other people who struggle with both their eating and their relationships. And most of us are unaware of how the two issues connect.

LAYING THE GROUNDWORK

It's important at this point in the book that I lay the groundwork for what's ahead. At times as you read the material here, you may find yourself asking, *What does this have to do with food?* At other times you may say to yourself, *What does this have to do with love?*

Remember, this is not a diet book. It's also not a relationship book. Rather it's my attempt to share with you the connection between the two in a way that may give you a breakthrough in both areas. Again, let me preface the following material by saying that this connection is not the only answer for these issues. Rather it's a piece of the puzzle. For some people—like me and many others—it's a very important piece. But let's keep it in perspective.

As a counselor I am aware that many factors besides food can affect our emotional health. Likewise numerous issues besides our emotional health are at work in our relationships. And clearly the state of our relationships is only one reason our health may be in decline.

Still, the information here changed my life, and I believe very strongly that most of us have overlooked this material for far too long. That said, let's take a little more in-depth look at the connection as I saw it play out in my life and the lives of so many others I've counseled.

What We Already Know about Food

There's no doubt about this truth: What we eat affects our physical health. If we eat a healthy, balanced, low-fat, low-sugar diet, we will have leaner bodies, less disease, and longer life as a general rule. Likewise if we eat a diet high in fat, sugar, and chemical additives (most of the nonfood ingredients listed on the labels of packaged food), we will have overweight bodies, more disease, and shorter life. This is not true for all people, but on the average it is common knowledge. In fact, this information has been around for decades even though most people with eating problems haven't paid much attention to it.

I know I didn't.

That said, this book will not focus on the information most of us already know. Instead, we will venture into new territory and examine how these same foods affect our emotions.

Remember the diagram of the cycle (SEE FIGURE 2):

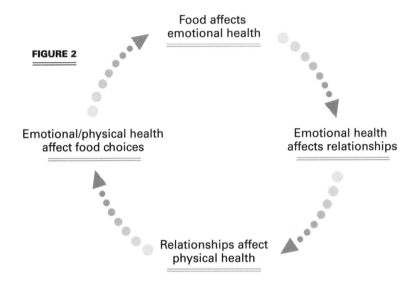

FIGURE 2

Food affects
emotional health

Emotional health
affects relationships

Relationships affect
physical health

Emotional/physical health
affect food choices

Before we start our discussion about food and its impact on our lives, I want to share a word picture that might help explain this connection. I own a chain saw. Last year, when I was getting ready to trim some trees, I filled the saw with the necessary gas and oil. But I was in a hurry and inadvertently poured gasoline in the oil reservoir and oil in the gasoline reservoir.

Unaware of my mistake, I turned on the switch and pulled the start cord to start the saw. I pulled and pulled and pulled. I tried everything and couldn't figure it out. Oh, it sputtered some, but nothing I could do would make it start! I was so frustrated I called a friend and asked how to start the thing. He talked me through the process, which was pretty much what I had done, but *that* didn't work either.

Finally, I opened up both the oil and gas lids, looked inside, and realized that I had poured the two fuels in the wrong reservoirs. So I dumped out the gas and oil, put the right fuel in the right reservoir, and tried to start the saw again. I pulled and pulled and pulled. Pretty soon, it started, but it smoked, and it didn't run right. Why? Because residue from having the wrong product in the wrong reservoir remained in the engine.

And that story is a very good picture of our bodies and food. First, it reminds us that if our bodies are going to function properly, they need fuel. And that fuel is food.

"Well, that's pretty obvious," you may say. But think about it. When you eat, do you think about the fuel, or do you think about the taste or the quantity or the look of the food? Many of us don't really see food as a necessary fuel. We see eating food as something we do when we get together with friends or colleagues at noon. It's what we do when we want to celebrate or spend time with friends. We eat certain foods because they look good, they taste good, or we want an emotional pick-me-up—not because they are the fuel our bodies need.

Second, my chain-saw story is a picture of how our bodies react when we fill them with the wrong fuel. They just don't work right. Then, even after we realize our mistake and put the correct fuel in, our bodies sputter for a while as they clean themselves out.

So as you read the upcoming chapters, remember that the fuel you put into your body makes all the difference in how your body—as well as your emotions and relationships—will function.

Our Food Choices Affect Our Emotional Health

Many factors play a role in our emotional health. Certainly our family history, health history, job status, and relationships all affect our emotional health. But one factor I overlooked most of my life was that food can affect our emotional health, our moods. My own experience and the experience of thousands of people I surveyed demonstrate that when we eat certain foods, various emotional states tend to follow on a consistent basis. While this may not be the case for you, it's worth considering.

Foods high in fat, sugar, and chemical additives may contribute to a host of negative emotions, while foods rich in nutrients—fresh fruits and vegetables, grains, and lean meats—may contribute to positive emotions. I'll explain this observation more fully in part 2, but for now, let's look at depression as an example. Obviously, many people who suffer from depression do so because of a chemical imbalance or because of specific circumstances in their lives. But let's say poor food choices have led to weight gain or illnesses that result in isolation or irritability. And that, in turn, has perhaps contributed to a poor self-image. It is very possible, then, that these factors may make a person depressed. And there is growing scientific evidence that some depression may be caused by the foods we eat.[1]

The reverse may also be true.

People who make healthy food choices and have a strong self-image will most likely be more joyful. This may even be true if they have a tendency toward depression.

Our Emotional Health Affects Our Relationships

Perhaps this next step in the cycle is as obvious to you as it was to me. I knew without a doubt that my negative emotions affected the way I related to my family and friends. What I didn't know was that food had contributed to those emotions.

If people exhibit uncontrolled anger, pessimism, anxiety, or bad moods on a regular basis, their relationships are bound to be affected. People with these emotional traits will be more likely to have conflicts with their spouses, children, and even coworkers.

On the other hand, if people are generally ruled by joy, peace, patience, and a positive attitude, their relationships are bound to be stronger. Again, this information is probably not surprising. What is a surprise is that the foods you eat may indirectly be affecting the way you get along with the people you love.

Our Relationships Affect Our Physical Health

The person who really helped me see the connection between our relationships and our physical health is Dr. Dean Ornish, internationally known cardiologist. In his book *Love and Survival*, Ornish says, "The health of people who have intimate, close, caring relationships are drastically better off than those who don't."[2] Just as common sense tells us that foods affect our physical health, most of us also know that our relationships affect our emotional health. The segment of the cycle we may not have known is that our relationships affect our *physical* health. Numerous studies released in the past five years prove that people with poor and/or limited relationships and social connections are more likely to have poor physical health. Similarly, people with strong and/or numerous relationships and social connections are more likely to have good physical health. Part 4 will give you some research about this.

How does this relate to the connection between food and love?

It works like this: Foods affect our emotions, emotions affect our relationships, and relationships affect our physical health. Therefore, the food choices we make—whether good or bad—may very well play a role in our relationships, as well as our physical and emotional health.

Our Emotional and Physical Health Affect Our Food Choices
That brings us to the last piece of the connection. Our emotional and physical health affect our food choices. Let me give you a picture of how this looks. When people suffer from poor emotional and physical health, they are in a sense like walking wounded. Because of that, they have what I call "holes in their hearts," holes caused by unhappiness and unmet needs from past relationships.

I believe that God designed us to have those "holes" filled by himself, but most people find other ways to fill the holes in their lives. They often turn to quick-and-easy substitutes.

Food ranks high among them.

And so the cycle is complete. Our food choices affect our emotional health; our emotional health affects our relationships; our relationships affect our physical health; and our emotional and physical health affect our food choices.

I think it's important for us to see the word *choices* here. If we choose healthy foods, we are in the best possible position to have healthy bodies and healthy relationships. If we choose unhealthy foods, we make ourselves vulnerable to having unhealthy bodies and unhealthy relationships, which can lead us to even more unhealthy food choices. And I'm very aware that the choices may not be in your control. As I mentioned earlier, most people want to make healthy choices regarding their bodies and relationships, but they lack either the knowledge or the willpower to do so.

WHY A RELATIONSHIP GUY IS WRITING THIS BOOK
A friend of mine mentioned to a group of medical personnel that I was writing a book on the power of food and relationships, and how one affected the other. One of the doctors in the group wrinkled his brow and scratched his head. "Gary Smalley? Isn't he that relationship guy?"

Some of you also may be wondering why a "relationship guy" would be writing a book about food and love. The answer is clear: I'm constantly seeing the connection between food and love in the lives of the people I counsel and the people who attend my seminars, and I've begun to learn that the better our relationships are, the healthier we are in general. The more we extend love to one another, the more likely we will find freedom from poor food choices and other poor health habits.

The bottom line is this: Food affects our relationships more than we've ever realized before. It's an aspect of relationship education that for me has been missing for decades. And it was a lack of understanding in these areas that placed a strain on my relationships with my family and friends.

I am confident that the information in this book will be enough to propel you to lasting change. In the next chapter you will find three short tests that will help you determine your physical and relational health.

I'm so excited about this information that I want to share it with anyone who will listen. Why? Because certain foods and unhealthy habits may actually be strangling your relationships. At the same time, if your spouse or someone you love is trapped by overeating and excess weight, your lack of a loving response is doing additional damage to that person's physical health—and yours—and is possibly increasing his or her emotional need to eat.

This book will also give you sound advice from several physicians and nutritionists, including Rex Russell, a nutrition expert who has found scriptural answers to food questions. In addition to learning ideas that may bring about lasting change in your life, you will be given several options for eating in a new way, a way that may improve all aspects of your life.

It worked for me, and I'm happy to tell you it worked for Barbara. It's also worked for countless others who have improved both their health and their relationships by implementing the facts laid out in the following chapters.

Now it can work for you.

But it won't work if you look only to your own strength or willpower to make it happen.

Most of us already know what we should be doing to improve our relationships, but we lack the desire and the power to implement the change. Likewise, we know what we should be eating, but we actually like foods that weaken our immune systems. Many of us, like Barbara, are overweight and have failed at every attempt to rid ourselves of the problem. We know our weight is affecting our marriage and our health, but we feel we can't do anything to fix the problem.

As my own journey illustrates, a strategy dependent on our own abilities will almost certainly fail. Only when we tap into God's strength, into his power, will we gain both the desire and ability to improve our relationships and our eating habits.

Reading this book could change your life. Your hope will soar as I share with you the simple steps to accessing godly inner power and developing the lasting changes you want in your relationships and eating habits.

I pray it does.

CHAPTER THREE

Take the Tests

Caroline knew she needed help the day the scale told her she had hit three hundred pounds. It was a moment that came just weeks after her husband, Jack, mentioned that he was getting frustrated with the lack of progress in their marriage and that maybe it was time to start talking about separation and possibly divorce. After all, everything loving and physical about their relationship had died long ago. They were little more than managers of a household in which physical touch seemed almost forbidden.

That afternoon after stepping on the scales and watching the needle make a full circle, Caroline locked herself in her bedroom and wept. What had happened? Why had their marriage become loveless? And why was she unable to stop eating foods she knew were destroying her?

"Help me, God," she cried out loud. "I'm at the end of my rope. I've done everything I know to do, and I'm all out of answers!"

Life hadn't always been this way, and that afternoon Caroline allowed herself to go back, back to her childhood days, when she was the only one of eight siblings who didn't struggle with weight problems. In fact, when Caroline was younger, she could easily eat sweets or breads all day long and never gain an extra pound.

Caroline had been especially close to her mother, and at a very young age their bond seemed somehow connected to the fact that like her mom, Caroline was thin. Caroline knew she was special, and she suspected it was because of her size.

Years passed, and although her siblings still struggled with their weight, Caroline enjoyed a metabolism that seemed to defy the odds. She ate the same junk food everyone else in her family ate, but because she was happy and busy, she probably ate less of it.

The happy days continued during college, when Caroline dated

Jack, whom she had known since high school. Although they had a solid relationship, Jack would sometimes say things that made her alarmed. "Caroline, I have just one doubt about our getting married. If you turn out like your sisters, it'll be hard for me to keep loving you."

Even with that niggling doubt, Jack and Caroline got married after they graduated, and during the first several years of their marriage, Caroline was able to remain thin—like her mother.

Things changed when Caroline got pregnant with their first baby. Almost from the beginning her body's chemistry seemed to change. When she visited the doctor, she showed weight gains of ten and twelve pounds a month during times when little or no gain was expected. The doctor warned her that anything in excess of twenty pounds would be difficult to shed, but Caroline felt helpless to stop the piling weight.

For the first time in her life she was worried about her looks. Everything good about her life—the attention she had always gotten, the love she had received from her husband—seemed connected to her weight. When she started getting heavy, she grew anxious and frustrated.

The more anxious and frustrated she grew, the more she ate. It was almost as if she was using food as a drug, a comfort. The worse she felt about herself, the more she turned to food.

Jack made matters worse by giving her casual warnings at first and finally outright criticisms. When she was just ten pounds overweight, he would joke that the baby better be big. But after Caroline had gained thirty pounds, he began showing her less affection. They kissed less, held hands less, and talked less. The love they had always shared together was gone almost overnight.

When he wasn't saying mean things, he was acting them out. Caroline remembers one night when she was six months pregnant and tried to snuggle up to Jack and kiss him. Instead, her husband turned his back and perched himself on his side of the bed. "I can't stand the way your fat feels against my skin," he said.

His words stung Caroline's heart. She began to hide what she ate. The pattern was fairly simple. She would tolerate Jack's comments by day, eating small servings and avoiding foods that were high in fat and sugar. When night came, she would explain that she had things to do, and she would let her husband go to bed alone. Then she would tear into the cupboards, the freezer, or wherever she had stored her secret stash, and she would eat for sometimes an hour straight.

Caroline was always surprised at the quantities she could consume in that hour—whole packages of cookies, half-cartons of ice cream, a box of Pop Tarts. She would eat until she could barely stand up, then she would tidy up her mess. She would stuff her wrappers inside paper bags or at the bottom of the trash can and rearrange her hiding places so no one knew the difference.

The cycle continued for years, through Caroline's second, third, and fourth pregnancies—until the day the scale registered three hundred pounds. That afternoon, when she had stopped crying and remembering the past, she realized an important truth: Never in all her life had she felt loved for who she was.

Suddenly Caroline realized that her mom had loved her because she was thin, her church friends had loved her because she volunteered her time, and her husband loved her because she had an attractive figure. Now that she was not thin, too busy with children to be involved at church, and no longer attractive physically, she felt completely unloved.

That's when I met Caroline. Her road back to healthy food choices and a healthy marriage relationship was a slow one, but she chose to break the cycle. Leaning on God for strength and comfort, she and Jack started to reverse the destructive spiral. If you saw Caroline on the street today, you would never guess that she once had weighed three hundred pounds.

Believe me, I see people like Caroline all the time. They illustrate the principles that are only now beginning to be taught by nutrition experts. Wrong food choices affect our relationships or the way we love; this then affects our health and leaves a void that we too often fill with wrong foods.

Now it's time to see if you also are caught in this cycle.

DO YOU NEED A CHANGE?

How can you catch a glimpse of your physical and relational health? Below I've created three tests to determine where you are and where you're headed. My guess is that how well you do on one test will correlate with how well you do on the others. The reason is the connection between food and love—whether good or bad. How much do you need to change—physically and relationally?

Take the following tests and see for yourself.

The Food Test

____1. I avoid foods such as frozen entrees, precooked and flavored chicken, breaded fish, lunch meats, or hot dogs.

____2. I eat foods such as broiled fish, plain chicken, or lean red meats that are free from additives.

____3. I avoid eating at fast-food restaurants.

____4. I eat a variety of raw fruits.

____5. I avoid white breads, pastries, hamburger buns, dinner rolls, or sandwich breads.

____6. I eat whole grain breads or whole grain cereals.

____7. I avoid deep-fried foods.

____8. I eat raw vegetables or raw vegetable juices.

____9. I avoid dairy products such as artificially flavored yogurt, full-fat sour cream, ice cream, and full-fat yellow cheese.

____10. I eat products that do not have added sugar, chemicals, or high fat content.

____11. I avoid sugar and foods that contain sugar (soft drinks, chocolate, candy, pastries, cookies, sugary condiments).

____12. I eat a variety of raw or unprocessed nuts.

Add up your points, and write your score here: _____.

SCORE 51–60: Congratulations! You have a very good understanding of healthy eating and probably do not struggle with many of the food-related issues other people struggle with. It is also likely that you will score well in the next two tests and that you are caught up in a positive cycle in the connection between food and love. It is still important that you understand the connection—both positively and negatively as it's very possible that someone you love may be struggling with food choices.

SCORE 38–50: You are better than average in your understanding of healthy food choices. Because of this your struggles with food-related issues are not as obvious as they might otherwise be. However, you may still have some significant issues with the connection between food and love. Take the next two tests to determine whether you do.

SCORE 25–37: Many of your food choices are poor ones, but your lifestyle still may not be drastically affected by this. Your greatest struggles with food and love may be internal, and though they may seem small to others, they threaten to be problems for you. It's possible that you are desperately in need of change but have been unable to see the connection between food and love or are unwilling to take a hard look at the issues.

SCORE 12–24: If there were a warning light on the panel of your life, the light would be flashing wildly, advising you to consider a change quickly. If you fall into this category, your relationships are clearly not the only area in danger of disaster. Depending on how long you've camped in this section of the testing grounds, see your doctor to make sure you aren't dealing with more than unhealthy food choices.

The Love Test

SCORING: In the space before each statement, write the number that applies to your situation:

1 = never
2 = rarely
3 = occasionally
4 = frequently
5 = every day

____1. I express my love physically to my spouse (touching, hugging, holding hands, kissing).

____2. I express my love physically to the other people I love (touching, hugging).

____3. I am able to demonstrate patience with the people around me.

____4. I am able to communicate my feelings to my spouse.

____5. I am involved in caring social relationships outside my home.

____6. I strengthen my ability to love by praying and reading the Bible.

____7. I am generally optimistic.

____8. I share my deepest needs with my spouse.

Add up your total points, and write your score here: _____.

SCORE 31–40: You are blessed with wonderful relationship skills. As a result you are more likely to live longer, avoid illness and disease for many decades, and enjoy good health and energy. Your relationships are so fulfilling that you probably make good food choices and avoid harmful habits. If you do struggle with such habits on any level, you readily will be open to change.

SCORE 21–30: Your relationship skills are better than most. There's a good chance you understand the importance of communication and physical touch in a marriage. Because of that, your chances of getting sick or turning to unhealthy eating habits are moderate.

SCORE 8–20: Your relationship skills need work. As a result you are at a higher risk for illness and disease. You may feel that your emotional life is not what it could be and that it is getting worse all the time. Or you may compare yourself to others and know that your marriage and other relationships are in need of constructive change. You may often make poor food choices or engage in harmful habits to comfort yourself from the pain of knowing life could be better. The resulting conflicts chafe at your heart and can be the cause of illness and disease.

The Food-Love Connection Test

SCORING: In the space before each statement,
write the number that applies to your situation:

1 = never
2 = rarely
3 = occasionally
4 = frequently
5 = always

____1. During or after a busy day, I find myself eating snacks made of sugar, chocolate, or fatty products.

____2. When I'm feeling bad about something, I eat unhealthy foods.

____3. I try to lose weight, but I end up failing.

____4. I feel guilty most of the time about how I eat.

____5. I eat food for comfort or out of boredom.

____6. I eat when I'm not hungry.

____7. I hide the food I eat from my spouse or other people.

____8. I am critical of myself or my spouse regarding food choices.

____9. I am critical of myself or my spouse regarding excess weight.

____10. I believe food and health issues have damaged my marriage or other key relationships.

____11. When I am feeling down or depressed, upset, bored or lonely, I don't feel like exercising.

Add up your total points, and write your score here: _____.

SCORE 11–25: You have a good understanding of healthy eating habits and a grasp on what it is to eat and view food in a way that will benefit both your body and your marriage or other relationships. Still, there may be inconsistencies. This could be caused by one of two reasons. First, you might be operating in your own strength and perhaps have been blessed with an extraordinary amount of self-control. However, because you are operating in your own strength, you may find that you are inconsistent about making healthy choices. Second, your slight lack of strength in this area could be caused by underlying trouble in your relationships.

SCORE 26–40: Too often you live life in the mire of mediocrity when it comes to your physical and emotional health. This may be because you are operating in your own strength. Most likely you have tried and failed at making improvements in your overall health. You may be perpetually down on yourself about health and food issues. This, in turn, may be affecting your marriage so that it is not what it once was or can be. You may have learned how to exist this way, but inside your heart you know there's a better life out there somewhere, and you want it for yourself.

SCORE 41–55: You are in serious need of change, both physically and relationally. A person who has fallen into the trap of living the lifestyle described in the eleven statements above, will have little time for healthy relating. Instead, you most likely spend your time seeking wrong foods, trying to avoid wrong foods, or feeling guilty about eating them. This lifestyle will take a serious toll on your marriage and other relationships, if it hasn't already. In addition, it can lead to a weakened immune system if left unchecked.

HOW DID YOU DO?

Now that you've had a chance to evaluate yourself in three areas, sit back and take a look at the results. Although these tests are not definitive and other factors certainly play a part in all three areas, I believe at this point you have a better understanding of how important the connection between food and love is in your life.

If you scored fairly well on all three sections, congratulations! You may have a better working knowledge of the connection between food and love than you ever realized. Still, it's quite possible that you have struggled with food choices or aspects of your relationships at some point and may need the information in this book to prevent additional trouble down the road. In addition, someone you love may be experiencing far greater problems than you are. If that's the case, finish this book and pass it on to that person. If he or she is not open to reading a book like this, pray for the person. Either way, the information here will help you better understand the connection between food and love.

If your score was average, keep in mind that most of us are not in a holding pattern. Generally our overall health, both physically and emotionally, is on the incline or decline. Use the results to help you find areas that may soon be real trouble for you or to recognize areas where you have recently improved. Then as you read the material here, take special notice of how the connection between food and love affects you personally.

Was your score lower than you would like? If so, then this book is especially for you. Perhaps, like me, you've never recognized the connection between food and love and how easy it is to be caught in a negative cycle involving both areas of your life. This is not a time to be discouraged. This book is full of hope for people like you and me. Read on and remember, your breakthrough in eating and relating to others may be just ahead.

PART **2**

OUR FOOD CHOICES AFFECT
OUR EMOTIONAL HEALTH

CHAPTER FOUR

Foods That Threaten
Our Emotional Health

Now that you've taken the tests and have a better sense of where you are personally, let's look at food and how it affects us. As I mentioned in previous chapters, we already know how foods can harm or help our physical health. During the past decades countless studies have proven that high-fat foods contribute to heart disease, that caffeine can leave us jittery, that foods high in sugar can cause us to gain weight, that salt affects our blood pressure—and a whole list of other correlations. Research in these areas gave us this cliché: "You are what you eat."

I would like to introduce a new concept: "You *feel* what you eat."

In this chapter we'll take a look at foods that have been linked to poor emotional health. If you find yourself struggling in your relationships or with your emotions, take a good hard look at this list. Maybe you'll find the connection between food and love at work in your own life.

NONE OF US IS A PERFECT EATER

My daughter, Kari, recently said to me, "Dad, living in the real world with my kids' going to birthday parties, class parties, and holiday celebrations and all, they're going to eat some things that aren't good for them. I mean, they're going to have chocolate cake."

As I listened to her, I thought, *Chocolate cake! That contains several foods that I know are harmful to my grandchildren.*

Then she added, "They won't do this all the time, but once in a while they are going to have junk food."

She brings up a good point.

I've come to realize that none of us will be a perfect eater. The way we eat will always fall somewhere between very healthy and very unhealthy.

However, by understanding how to operate in God's strength, we can achieve a degree of freedom that will enable us to come closer to the healthy side of eating far more often. This, then, will improve our physical health and very likely improve our emotional health in a way that may greatly improve our relationships.

Perhaps this will be easier to understand if we think of our health on a continuum from 0–100. When we eat very healthy foods, we fall somewhere close to the high end of the continuum, near 100. When we eat unhealthy foods, we will fall somewhere close to the low end, near 0:

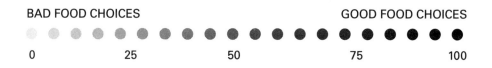

BAD FOOD CHOICES   GOOD FOOD CHOICES

0   25   50   75   100

From all I've read about food, the highest level of health results from a diet of organic raw fruits and vegetables; nuts and grains; and some lean meats and fish. A diet with fewer fruits, vegetables, nuts and grains, and more red meat scores somewhere closer to 75. A diet that includes lots of processed foods puts us below 50. And eating lots of chemically enhanced foods—such as most boxed foods, lunch meats with nitrates, many packaged snack foods—or foods that are high in sugar, marinated, or fried move us closer to the 25 to 0 range.

The reality is, your food choices will place you somewhere between 0 and 100.

If you're having doughnuts every day and if you regularly eat fried and processed foods with chemical additives, you will be at the extreme, worst end. If you eat only raw vegetables and fruits, grains and nuts, and lean proteins, you will be at the extreme, healthy end of the spectrum.

Remember my earlier story about the chain saw? The word picture applies here again. If we put the wrong fuel into our bodies, they will malfunction, moving us closer to the 0—the ineffective end of the continuum.

So, where are you on the spectrum? Where would you like to be?

The choice is really up to you.

It may help you to think of your choices as one of these options:

- I would like to be physically and emotionally more healthy.
- I don't really care; I'll be somewhere in the middle.
- I really want to be unhealthy.

None of us knowingly makes the decision to be unhealthy. The problem is that while we want to live at the high end of the continuum, we often don't have the willpower to stop eating foods that place us at the low end.

This book will help you understand how to tap into God's power in order to make your positive choice a reality. The closer you get to 100, the better you'll look and feel, and the better you will relate to the people around you.

BE ENCOURAGED

Remember, if you have an ice-cream cone at your family reunion, you aren't a failure. Your food choice simply pushes you down the continuum that day. That's okay; it's a choice.

The point is this: I don't always eat perfectly, and neither do you. I'm still learning as I go through life, still listening for God's direction and seeking his help. I say this to encourage you not to feel defeated before you ever even gain the power to change your eating habits. It's a day-to-day process of learning and gaining power from God to do it.

The benefits of choosing a healthier diet will be amazing. Not only will you most likely lose weight, you may also experience the emotional benefits we're about to discuss. You'll read more about this later, but let me say here that what has thrilled me most about this new way of eating unprocessed, whole foods is that I can eat a lot of it and not gain a pound. I'm also not hungry all the time, as I was before.

As you continue reading, I would like you to see the overall benefits of eating a healthier diet, a diet closer to the one God laid out for us in the Bible. Follow along, and allow yourself to get excited. Allow God to use this as a time of breakthrough in your life—even though it may not kick in immediately.

Yes, food choices make up just one aspect of healthy relationships. But it's one we've overlooked for too long. Recognize that it's possible for God to show you the truth about what you eat and how it affects not only your emotions and consequently your relationships, but also your relationship with him.

FOUR FOODS THAT AFFECT OUR EMOTIONAL HEALTH

It's important that you clearly understand what the following paragraphs and the next chapter will say about the connection between food and love.

The idea that what we eat affects our emotions is certainly one being discussed in current medical research.[1] It was also very true of my experience and the experiences of thousands of people I've counseled or talked with at seminars.

I would like to be able to tell you that the television commercials are right, that candy bars will sustain your energy and make you happy and popular among your peers. Or that after a diet of pizza and potato chips, you can play a friendly game of touch football and feel at your physical and emotional best.

And maybe for some of you, the commercials ring true. You can eat whatever you want and never notice the negative affects on either your physical or emotional health.

However, the truth for most people—at least as far as I can tell—is something quite different. What I've found is that people who make poor food choices are vulnerable to a range of negative emotional responses that can affect their relationships. Conversely, people who make good food choices are more likely to have positive emotional responses, which put them in a better position to have healthy relationships.

One reason this seems to be true is because nutritionists have proven that many foods have been stripped of the nutrients that might otherwise feed the brain. When the brain is lacking proper nutrients, our emotions are directly affected in a negative way.[2]

I want to try to make this simple. The remainder of this chapter will take a look at the four poorest food choices a person might make. Remember the continuum we looked at earlier in this chapter? The foods detailed here are the ones that will put you on the far left. Obviously, there will be times when we will eat these foods.

The goal is to move as far to the right on the continuum as possible and to do this as many days of the week as possible. Kay Sheppard's book *From the First Bite: A Complete Guide to Recovery from Food Addiction* explains that in doing so, you may see a tremendous difference in your emotional health and moods.[3]

FOODS THAT WEAKEN OUR BODIES AND LOVE

Foods can have an effect on our emotions. The wrong kinds of foods can threaten our emotional health. For instance, even a small amount of processed food or caffeine can actually alter the chemical balance in our brains and cause mood changes.

If your energy level is low and you find you don't do things with your spouse, children, or friends as a result, the foods you eat may be contributing to your lack of energy.[4] My research indicates that common ailments such as muscle and joint stiffness or soreness, headaches, colds, sore throats can be caused by the food—the fuel—that we put into our mouths. The more I read, the more I see that many of the foods we eat—foods that look good, smell good, and taste good—are really counterfeit foods. They don't have the nutrients our cells need to grow and keep us healthy.

Let's get a little more specific. The following paragraphs will discuss foods that weaken us—in other words foods that affect our emotional health and ultimately our relationships. Relax, find a quiet place, and read this with an open mind, an open heart.

I know what you're thinking: *Oh no! He's going to say sugar is bad!* You're right. That's what I'm going to say. Except I will go even further.

All refined and processed foods are destructive. What do I mean by refined and processed foods? They are foods in which the life-giving nutrients have been stripped and diminished in the refining process. The result is a product that lasts long on the shelf and perhaps even tastes good. But it is also a product proven to be very harmful to our health.

Take a look at the following list of the four poorest food choices, all of which are refined and processed. These four foods are the biggest culprits in harming our emotional and physical health.[5]

1. White or refined sugar
2. White or refined flour
3. Hydrogenated oils and animal fat
4. Chemically laden foods

By the way, the next chapter will list the nutritious foods that you can use instead of these four harmful foods. Now let's take a look at these foods individually and understand why they harm our health and affect our moods.

White or Refined Sugar

Refined sugar is harmful to our health. In her book *Food Smart!* nutritionist Cheryl Townsley asserts, "I believe that white flour and white sugar are as lethal as cocaine. As much as you can, eliminate these white powders." She goes on to say, "Sugar was a big contributor to my emotional and mental problems. . . . Reducing our sugar intake can have as many signs of withdrawal as quitting drugs."[6]

She quotes Dr. John Yudkin, a physician and biochemist who taught at London University, as saying, "If only a fraction of what is already known about the effects of sugar were to be revealed in relation to any other material used as a food additive, that material [sugar] would be banned."[7]

In her book *Lick the Sugar Habit,* Nancy Appleton lists eighty-seven reasons why sugar is dangerous for our health. A few of those reasons are that it can harm our immune system, cause headaches, cause weak eyesight, cause kidney damage, emphysema, multiple sclerosis, and aging. It can increase the risk of cancer and cause hormonal and brain imbalances. It can make our bones and tendons more brittle.[8] The list is depressingly long. (For another list see chapter 18, "Frequently Asked Questions.")

Numerous researchers have proven that diabetes is caused when the body's response to excess sugar causes the pancreas to wear out. And that's just one of the deadly diseases common among people who eat refined sugar and foods with a high sugar content.

In addition, sugar has been proven to affect our behavior, attention span, and learning abilities. This can be most easily seen by observing children before and after lunch at any school across America. The lunches of many children contain junk foods that are easy to pack in a box lunch but that are loaded with sugar. Nutritionist William Sears says that in general
a person's behavior, attention span, and learning abilities deteriorate in proportion to the amount of white sugar products they eat.[9]

The catch is that sugar can make us feel great—temporarily. In fact it activates in our brain beta-endorphins that serve as painkillers initially. In fact in the mid 1980s Dr. Elliott Blass, now a researcher at Cornell University, conducted experiments that even looked at the possibility of using refined sugar as a legitimate painkiller. In the experiment scientists exposed mice to a dangerous level of floor heat. Mice exposed to sugar prior to the experiment took twice as long to lift their paws in response to the heat.[10] Other studies by Blass proved that sugar initially also dulled emotional pain.

No wonder people turn to sugar to ease the pain in their hearts, the pain caused by poor love. Again, we see the cycle between food and love in action.

By the way, the reason scientists decided not to use sugar as a painkiller is because it works only for a short time. Some thirty minutes to an hour after consuming sugar, physical and emotional pain actually intensify.

White or Refined Flour

White and refined flours are made by taking whole grains, pulverizing them, and sifting out the germ and any fiber content. The result is a soft powdery substance that is great to bake with—but terrible for our health. Nutritionists explain that "26 essential nutrients, plus bran, have been removed from wheat to produce white bleached flour."[11]

When we eat flour, it is absorbed into the bloodstream through the walls of the stomach and small intestine. The more refined the flour—and white bleached flour is the most refined—the more quickly this process takes place. The more quickly flour is absorbed into the bloodstream, the more dramatic the effect it has on our brain chemistry and the more quickly it may alter our moods.[12]

Some nutritionists say that the most dramatic effect refined flour has on our moods is its ability to make us numb and mentally confused.[13] It is easy to see how feeling this way would be harmful to our relationships.

Hydrogenated Oils and Animal Fat

Processed oils and foods high in fat are also destructive. A processed oil is any oil that has been hydrogenated (hydrogen is added to the molecules) or processed with heat. Again, essential nutrients are lost in the processing, making most oils "empty" if not destructive foods.

Similarly, foods high in saturated fat will almost always contribute to poor health. They increase the chance of fatty plaque buildup in the major arteries, a troubling problem that occurs in a high percentage of Americans. This plaque buildup can then lead to high blood pressure and a higher risk of heart disease and sudden heart attacks.

Obviously, illness brought on by unhealthy food choices creates an emotional impact that is destructive in relationships. The person who eats himself or herself to a place of illness will feel more anxious, pessimistic, isolated, and frustrated. This person will most likely also suffer from a poor self-image, which can then lead to other emotional trouble.

In addition, hydrogenated oils—oils that are processed with heat—cause an immediate release of blood sugar in our systems, followed by the inevitable drop in our blood-sugar level. This drop can lead to bad moods, irritability, impatience, pessimism, mental confusion, and anxiety. Over time this kind of drop can contribute to more serious emotional conditions such as depression.[14]

Other fats that are harmful to our bodies are the animal fats found in meat and poultry. For the most part this is the fat that can be trimmed away in beef and the fatty skin on turkey or chicken that can be removed. Try to avoid this kind of fat because it can collect in our arteries and lead to heart disease.

Meat fat works its way through the body much like hydrogenated, processed fats and will cause us to gain weight, feel sluggish, confused, and tired. This then alters both our self-esteem and our moods, making us irritable and depressed.[15]

Chemically Laden Foods

Because we live in a fast-paced world that values convenience, many of our foods are processed so that they will last longer or so that they will be ready to eat when we want them: frozen entrees, lunch meats, boxed foods, to name a few. Processing a food involves taking a natural food and treating it with heat, chemicals, or additives.

Labels on packaged foods often list such nonfood ingredients (you know the ones, the ingredients with the unpronounceable names) as preservatives, artificial flavors, artificial colors, and a whole host of other chemicals. And all of that is in addition to the processed "foods" such as flours, sugars, and oils.

This processing makes the product more marketable to stores and to consumers. If a store can purchase a crate of pudding packages that don't have to be refrigerated and will last up to two years on a shelf, there's little or no risk to the store. The consumer comes along and feels the same way. Just stock up the family pantry, and you'll have tasty treats for the kids' lunches for months. Right?

Wrong.

You'll have children—your most precious possessions—eating imitation food, lots of sugar, chemicals, and food dyes, then attempting to function properly in a classroom for hours. It's not surprising that so many of today's kids are being treated for hyperactivity.

In the end, processed foods often contain added sugar, salt, and fat. Many packaged breakfast cereals are a good example.

What's worse, according to Cheryl Townsley and other nutritionists,

foods full of processed ingredients provide the lowest level of appetite satisfaction. That means you have to eat more of these foods to create a feeling of
fullness. No wonder people are gaining weight at alarming rates. Nutritionists also tell us that many of these processed foods are addictive. If we wind
up addicted to the product, we'll buy more. It's a profit deal for the food
companies, and it's keeping the health care industry in big bucks as well.

Two of the most common chemical food additives are artificial sweeteners and caffeine.

As concerns have risen about sugar intake, the food industry—always
ready to please the customer—has responded by developing an ever-
increasing list of artificial sweeteners. Most nutritionists suggest that artificial sweeteners are even worse for us than refined sugar. Townsley's book
Food Smart! sums up the problem with these chemicals by assuring us that
when we eat any of the artificial sweeteners, we decrease the amount of
energy in the spleen and pancreas. The effect is a serious blow to a
person's mood and energy level; in other words they negatively affect a
person's emotional health.[16]

Although caffeine is a chemical that occurs naturally in certain food
products, it is equally bad for you.

Okay, I've said it. At this point some of you may want to close the
book and throw it across the room. You may be saying, "It's one thing to
take away my sugar and processed snacks, but don't even think about
touching my coffee."

Listen, I know about the coffee fad. I've seen the espresso stands in
grocery stores and at the lube-and-oil shops. But obviously God has this
issue of good health on your heart or you wouldn't be reading the book. So
let God work! Besides, remember the continuum. None of us will be perfect,
but from this point on let's at least be informed.

Just one cup of coffee—or any other beverage with caffeine such as some
soft drinks, some teas, or hot chocolate—can lower energy, constrict blood
vessels, cause headaches, increase blood pressure, increase blood sugar, cause
restless sleep, cause calcium and magnesium losses through urination, aggra-
vate stomach lining, cause nervousness, irritability, anxiety, and depression.
Have you heard enough? Note that some of these are emotional symptoms.

Go back over the list, and imagine the ways that those symptoms will
harm your relationships—your marriage, your friendships, your relationships with your children. Is it worth it? For one or more cups of a beverage
with caffeine?

A LIST OF POOR FOODS TO AVOID

For people who want a specific list of foods to avoid, here is a list of some of the most obvious ones because of the refined sugar, refined flour, and fat:

- Candy
- Brownies
- Pastries and doughnuts
- Coffee
- Cakes
- Cookies
- Potato chips
- Oiled and salted nuts
- Ice cream
- Meats with fat content above 7 percent
- Chicken skin
- Fried foods
- Products made with white flour (white bread, flour tortillas, etc.)
- Product with sugar as the first, second, third, or fourth ingredient on the label (note: manufacturers tend to hide sugar with words such as dextrose, maltose, high-fructose corn syrup, etc.)
- Packaged foods such as crackers, cookies, or snack items made from refined sugar or refined flour
- Packaged meals or food items with chemical ingredients (generally these are the items you don't recognize as food on the ingredient list)

If you are eating a diet made up primarily from that list of nonfoods, it might be time to ask God for a change. If you've done that and you're in the waiting period, don't make yourself feel guilty. Just be glad for this information. It's important to know the truth about what you're eating.

Here's a fact that might help: It takes only two weeks for your taste buds to change. Two weeks is no big deal when you consider that eliminating these items may help not only your physical health but the health of your marriage and other relationships as well.

THE CHOICE IS YOURS

But no one said your changes have to come overnight. What it comes down to is choices.

It's your choice whether you're sick of living an unhealthy life and whether you would like to explore the possibility that eating better might improve your relationships. If the information in this chapter is at all accurate, then we have another way of seeing that our food choices launch us in one of two directions: a positive cycle or a negative one. The positive cycle would look like figure 3, and the negative cycle would look like figure 4.

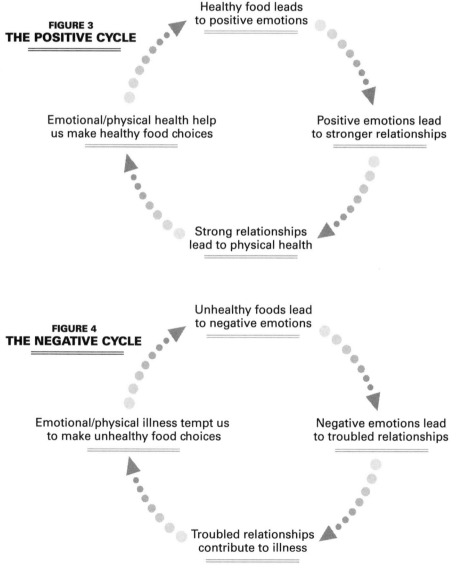

FIGURE 3
THE POSITIVE CYCLE

Healthy food leads
to positive emotions

Emotional/physical health help
us make healthy food choices

Positive emotions lead
to stronger relationships

Strong relationships
lead to physical health

FIGURE 4
THE NEGATIVE CYCLE

Unhealthy foods lead
to negative emotions

Emotional/physical illness tempt us
to make unhealthy food choices

Negative emotions lead
to troubled relationships

Troubled relationships
contribute to illness

It's your choice whether you want to take your decision to God and ask for his help. If you do that, if you expect him to answer you in a supernatural way, he will give you the strength and power to maintain the change when it happens! You will find the hope you've longed for. I'll help you understand more about this toward the end of the book.

WHERE DO YOU GO FROM HERE?

The bottom line is that I'm suggesting you stay away from these four categories of food: refined sugar, refined flour, hydrogenated oils and animal fat, and chemically laden foods. These foods will keep you at the left end of the continuum—the food choices that will place you close to a 0.

The good news is that for each category of poor food choices, there is a healthier food you can use instead. Get your appetites ready! The best foods are just ahead.

CHAPTER FIVE

Foods That Strengthen Our Emotional Health

or every negative emotional state that may be aggravated or even caused by poor food choices, there is a positive emotional state that could result from good food choices. Earlier I told you about how God used Dr. Rex Russell's book to give me the breakthrough I had been praying for. Russell's way of eating is very sound and scriptural, and it recommends food choices that may improve our emotional health. Research has proven that these same healthy foods may have a positive impact on our emotional health.[1] Our emotional health, remember, will have a direct impact on our relationships.

THREE PRINCIPLES FOR HEALTHY EATING

Let's take a look at the principles Russell suggests.

Principle 1: Eat only those foods and drinks God created for food. An obvious example is this: Oranges grow on a tree; they were created by God and are therefore of high nutritional value. Twinkies are created with processed foods and chemicals. They have a shelf life that exceeds decades in some cases. Therefore they were not created as food.

Principle 2: Eat foods in the state in which they were created to be eaten. Fresh bananas give you more nutrition than dried bananas or banana pudding. Raw carrots offer more real food to your body than freeze-dried carrots, carrots in a frozen entree, or carrot cake. Many foods we eat have been changed into another food form because the new form might last longer in a cupboard or freezer, or the food may be more convenient to prepare. Avoid processed foods. The more the food is processed—the more you heat food or add chemicals to it—the less benefit it has to your body.

Principle 3: Avoid food addictions. Do not let any food or drink become your god. If you do become addicted to a food, then fasting is one of the most powerful biblical remedies available. The reason? Because during your fast, you are restoring, renewing, and deepening your relationship with God and with people, which in turn gives you the energy to overcome the addiction you're in. This might mean fasting from a single type of food—say refined foods—or it might mean a fast that lasts twenty-four hours or longer. Be sure to check with your doctor before starting a fast that will last longer than a day.

In summary, Russell's eating formula is scriptural and quite simple. Eat natural fruits, vegetables, nuts, and grains. Eat lean meats, eggs, and some unprocessed dairy products. Avoid other foods that have been proven to be harmful, such as highly processed and refined foods or nonfood additives. And don't become dependent on certain foods. Eat whatever God created as natural, healthy food.[2]

FOODS THAT HELP US

Based on the understanding Rex Russell brings to us about nutrition, let's take a look at four alternatives to the poor food choices listed in the previous chapter.

1. Raw honey and sweeteners from raw fruit
2. Whole-grain flour and whole grains
3. Cold-pressed oils and healthy fats
4. Natural foods

As we did before, we'll take a look at each of these categories so we can better understand why they help our bodies both physically and emotionally.

Raw Honey and Sweeteners from Raw Fruit

The bad news is that white, refined sugar is harmful to our health. The good news is that God has provided the most natural sweetener of all: honey. Honey is five times sweeter than sugar! God tells us about honey in the Bible, advising us both to enjoy it and to be careful not to overeat it. Take a look at the following verses:

- "Eat honey, my son, for it is good; honey from the comb is sweet to your taste."

- "Kind words are like honey—sweet to the soul and healthy for the body."
- "If you find honey, eat just enough—too much of it, and you will vomit."
- "It is not good to eat too much honey."[3]

Interesting, isn't it, how God's instruction in the Bible is so reliable? Go ahead and eat honey—eat it from the comb (unprocessed). In fact it's got wonderful nutrients in it if you eat it raw and unprocessed. I buy it from a neighbor, who sells it raw with some of the honeycomb still in the jar.

Another natural sweetener is juice extracted from raw fruit. Fruit juice does not break down in the body as quickly as refined sugar. Because of that, our blood-sugar levels remain steady, thus helping our emotions to do the same.[4]

Fruit juices can be used as a sugar substitute to sweeten foods. For instance, when I make bread or muffins, I often use a few tablespoons of frozen 100 percent apple juice instead of refined sugar. Hot cereals can be sweetened with fresh fruit or juice from fresh fruit.

Whole-Grain Flour and Whole Grains

Most of you understand which foods are included in this category, but here's a refresher just in case you've forgotten. Grains include foods such as barley, rye, oats, brown rice, and wheat, among many others. Whole-grain flour can be made from any of those and used instead of refined, white flour.

The beauty of these natural grains is that they include the nutrients and fiber God intended us to eat. The result is that these grains are more slowly digested, causing a steady release of blood sugar, thereby regulating your brain function and your emotions at the same time.[5]

These items are rich with fiber, protein, good fats, and enzymes crucial to life and health. Again do some research, and learn about the different types of foods in this category.

Unlike vegetables, grains do not lose their nutritious value when they are cooked. Getting a good mix of grains in your diet will likely contribute to a release of energy. This in turn will almost always help elevate your mood.

Cold-pressed Oils and Healthy Fats

Most oils come from seeds that are crushed and pressed to extract the oil. Whenever possible, use these cold-pressed oils, which retain the nutrients of the food from which they are made. But be aware that most of the oils available in the supermarket have been extracted with heat, which removes many of the nutrients. Furthermore, heat-processed oils have also been refined with potentially toxic substances. These improve shelf life and make oil cheap to produce, but the resulting product becomes dangerous to your health.[6] Again, it will not be possible to avoid these types of oils all the time. Remember the continuum, and try to lean toward the right, avoiding these oils or foods that contain them whenever possible.

One way to eat healthy oils is to eat them in their natural state. A food that nutritionist William Sears says is on his top-ten list of foods is flax seeds, available in health-food stores. Flax seeds are especially helpful for brain function and thus emotional stability.[7] Other foods that will improve cellular health, brain function, and possibly emotional health include cold-pressed olive oil, canola oil, and soybean oil; avocados; olives; and peanut butter. By the way, many grocery stores are set up so you can grind your own peanuts, which means a healthier food with no added sugar or processing.

Natural Foods

Natural foods are a healthy alternative to foods that have been processed and that contain chemical additives. Natural foods, which are closest to the way God made them, include fresh fruits and vegetables; legumes, nuts, and seeds; seafood; poultry and eggs; and meats. My guess is that very little in this list will surprise you. But I want you to understand the benefits all the same.

You're probably familiar with the physical benefits of fresh fruits and vegetables. These include their natural vitamin and mineral content as well as their fiber—the material that is not digested but rather pushed through the stomach and intestines as a way of maintaining regular elimination.

That's the part most of us already know.

What you may not know is that many nutrients in fresh vegetables and fruits elevate moods and regulate blood sugar, consequently helping us to avoid or moderate irritability, uncontrolled anger, and depression.[8]

In addition, a diet rich in fresh fruits and vegetables will almost always help you lose weight or maintain a healthy body image. This, then, will also aid in improving your emotional health, as we will see in part 3.

Legumes are beans or lentils such as black beans, pinto beans, white beans, garbanzo beans, and split peas. Nuts and seeds include foods such as almonds, walnuts, pecans, peanuts, sunflower seeds, sesame seeds, and flax seed. These foods add fiber, nutrients, and protein to our diets, thereby feeding the brain and resulting in strong emotional health.[9]

Again, many factors contribute to our emotional health. But the foods you eat may be playing a larger role than you ever imagined.

One other benefit? Many of the people I've counseled have expressed a connection between "alive" foods (a diet with at least six fresh fruits and vegetables) and having a stronger sexual drive. Processed foods are "dead" and, well . . . you reach your own conclusion.

THE IMPORTANCE OF LEAN PROTEIN

Although it's important to avoid fatty meats, it's also crucial that we get ample lean protein every day.[10] Let me share with you a personal story that demonstrates the power of protein on our emotional health. At one point in my understanding about food, I was eating a mostly vegetarian diet—fruits and vegetables and very few beans, which contain protein. Overall, my protein intake was very low.

During that period I woke up one morning and realized my mood was really down. I was irritated and grouchy, and I ended up snapping at Norma. We were about to take a special vacation, but I was feeling miserable, moody, and upset with everything and everyone. I was literally feeling disgusted with life in general.

That afternoon Norma and I went to a restaurant, and I had a piece of chicken—lean, clean protein—for the first time in many months. In only a half an hour, my dark mood lifted, and my perspective changed dramatically. Why? The research I've done since that afternoon indicates that it was because I finally met my body's need for protein. By the time Norma and I walked out to the car, I was upbeat, laughing, and enthusiastic. I said, "Norma remind me to eat protein every day because I do not want to be grouchy anymore."

Not only was I hurting myself by not giving my body enough protein, but I was also hurting Norma and other people around me. That day I experienced the amazing connection between food and love in a dramatic way.

While it's true that most Americans are eating more protein than their bodies can use, it's important to remember the value in this necessary food. The Bible makes a great case for lean proteins from "clean" animals only.[11] The list of lean, clean, and healthy proteins, as it is derived from the Bible, includes beef, chicken, turkey, a variety of fowl, deer, goat, ox, and sheep. As it turns out, the same list is most heartily approved by nearly every nutritionist teaching on the topic today.

The Bible's list of acceptable foods does not include pig, rabbit, and other "unclean" four-legged animals. Here's an interesting fact: Every one of the animals listed in the Bible as unclean carried a higher risk of being diseased and of passing on that disease to humans. It is interesting how God's supposedly outdated Old Testament teaching on foods proves to hold modern-day truths that will benefit our health.

In 1953, David Macht did a study at Johns Hopkins University on the toxic effects of animal flesh on a controlled growth culture. Although he was not attempting to prove the truth of Bible passages written thousands of years earlier about animal food, that's exactly what his study did. A meat substance was classified as toxic if it slowed the culture's growth rate below 75 percent. The results were amazing in their support of the Bible. The flesh of every animal and fish given to us by God for food all proved to be nontoxic. But the forbidden animals as referenced in the Bible, all came up with toxic levels.[12]

You may know that protein is the building block that creates muscle and gives our bodies endurance. And perhaps the area protein most contributes to our emotional health is its ability to stabilize blood-sugar levels.

What you might not know is that when blood-sugar levels are out of balance, you may experience any of the following emotional symptoms: fatigue, irritability, mood swings, depression, anxiety, and low energy. These emotional states can contribute to more serious emotional conditions including uncontrolled anger and feelings of isolation.

In addition to lean proteins, including healthy fats such as cold-pressed oils, raw nuts, avocados, and olives in your diet may lead to improved emotional health. Although nutritionists advise people to keep their overall fat intake to no more than 30 percent of their overall food intake each day, research has also shown that these healthy fats play a role in improving our physical and emotional health.[13]

Are you beginning to understand how food and love are connected?

SIX BENEFITS TO HEALTHY EATING

The same four healthy food choices that may help our emotional health to be in tip-top shape also help our physical health. Most of you will be familiar with this information, but it's so valuable, it's worth listing here anyway.[14] When we eat nutritious foods in their natural state, we give our bodies the optimal chance of being healthy. It's this simple: When you give your body the right fuel, it will function effectively.

1. When you eat healthy foods, you generally will be sick less often.

2. When you eat healthy foods, you become healthier emotionally. Depression and mood swings can act like a pair of distortion glasses, altering every feeling and thought. Since these are affected negatively by wrong foods, it makes sense they would be affected positively by right foods.

3. As your emotional health improves, so does your ability to think clearly and behave consistently. A great place to see this in action is with grade-school children. When a positive change in diet is made, many children go from having erratic behavior and cognitive problems to calm, cooperative behavior. Obviously students learn better when exhibiting the latter.

4. When you eat healthy foods, you will experience physical benefits. These are almost too numerous to mention, but they include the ability to control your weight to whatever amount you want. (This happens best when eating lean proteins as well as fibrous fresh vegetables and fruits.) When your weight is under control, you will experience a better self-image and less self-loathing. This typically results in more social connectedness and less isolation.

5. You will sleep better when you're eating a diet made up mostly of fruits, vegetables, grains, lean proteins, and nuts. Reduce your caffeine intake, but if you do drink beverages with caffeine, don't do it in the evening.

6. When you eat healthy foods, your skin and eyes will look healthier. The reason for this is because your body is being cleansed by your better food choices.

In addition to these benefits, you will also see financial rewards. You'll probably save hundreds, even thousands of dollars in medical bills. Why? Because you won't need to buy as many medicines to address problems possibly caused by poor eating habits. Anne Frähm, author of *Cancer Battle Plan,* writes, "I spent more than $250,000 dying with cancer, but I spent less than $2,000 getting well by eating healthy."[15] A person who is sick less often is a person who usually benefits from good emotional health as well.

FOODS THAT ARE GOOD FOR YOUR BODY AND EMOTIONS

Now that we have discussed the categories of foods that may benefit your emotional health, let's look at a list of specific foods that you can include in your eating plan. Again, the more of these types of foods you eat, the closer you move toward the right on the continuum. And that remains the goal.

FRESH FRUITS. Again, eat fruits close to their raw, natural state. Wash off pesticides with a vegetable wash.[16] Eat a variety of apples, bananas, oranges, grapes, pears, cherries, kiwi, figs, plums, nectarines, tangerines, peaches, melons, strawberries, blueberries, blackberries, and raspberries.

FRESH VEGETABLES. Eat all varieties, as many colors and types as possible every day. Eat them as close to their raw, natural state as possible. Wash off pesticides with a vegetable wash. In addition to common vegetables such as leaf lettuce, tomatoes, cucumbers, carrots, green beans, corn, onions, broccoli, and potatoes, be sure to eat other vegetables such as kale, spinach, squash, asparagus, cauliflower, mushrooms, garlic, avocado, beets, and turnips.

LEAN CHICKEN. Broiled, skinless chicken is the most healthy.

FISH. Eat a variety of broiled salmon, all types of white fish, tuna, albacore, halibut, and the like.

LEAN BEEF. Small amounts of broiled beef are best.

WHOLE GRAINS. Eat whole grains as close to their raw state as possible. Eat a variety that includes oats, wheat, brown rice, millet, and barley.

RAW NUTS. While almonds are particularly good for you, eat a variety of unprocessed nuts.

RAW SEEDS. In addition to sunflower and sesame seeds, flax, as I mentioned earlier, is a wonderful food. Not only does it help your brain function, it also may help lower blood cholesterol.

LEGUMES. Add beans and lentils to your diet, including black beans, garbanzo beans, pinto beans, lentils, and peas.

SPROUTS. Sprouts are seeds that have grown into a green, salad-type product. Sprouts are very high in nutrients.

DRIED FRUITS. Include raisins, prunes, and dates in your diet, but make sure that they are dried without chemicals.

SOY PRODUCTS. Soy products have isoflavones, which may play a role in reducing cancer risks, particularly in women. Try to include soy milk, soy cheese, soy meat replacements, and soy protein powder or granules in your diet instead of their dairy and animal meat counterparts.

OLIVE OIL. While most people believe that oils are not healthy, cold-pressed olive oil is healthy for the body because it provides nutrients that are essential for all body functions.

ELEVEN WAYS TO GET STARTED

So, having read the list of foods to avoid and the foods to eat, you may be a little overwhelmed at the thought of changing your eating patterns. Don't be discouraged; give yourself some time. It takes thirty days to change a habit, and if you are serious about changing yours, these steps may help make the road toward change more manageable.

1. Start removing the refined and processed foods from your kitchen. Take an inventory of your cupboards and pantry. Take out refined sugar, the white flours, hydrogenated oils, and the chemically laden foods, which do not contain the enzymes and minerals your body needs.

2. Make a list of the healthy foods that you want to buy, and start stocking your kitchen with these new foods. Make sure you have whole grains of many different kinds. Purchase a variety of raw nuts. Regularly buy a variety of vegetables and fruits, colorful and as fresh as possible. Add lean protein foods such as eggs, chicken, and fish.

3. Keep a journal of what you're eating and how that is making you feel. Record miracles that God performs, especially if you've had an eating disorder or a food addiction.

4. Become informed. Don't believe the advertisements about how "good" certain foods at restaurants are. In other words, when you're buying a food—whether at a restaurant or at a grocery store—find out about the ingredients. When you are in a restaurant, ask about the ingredients in the

food. For products you buy in a store, read the labels and see what you're buying. For example, avoid buying any foods that have nitrates in them; lunch meats and other processed meats are the most likely candidates. Nitrates have clearly been linked to diseases such as cancer.

5. Ask God to give you the desire to eat the healthy foods.

6. Have smaller meals, and eat delicious snacks (smaller portions) of real food. Examples: fruits, nuts, raw vegetables, soy milk, or make your own muffins, granola, breads, and honey bars (natural).

7. Eat fruits in as natural a state as possible. In addition to munching on whole fruits, try making juice from them. For example, I make juice from the fruits that I love. I have a juicer that does this fairly well. I just put about two inches of homemade apple juice in the blender, add a few more fruits to that (like strawberries or blueberries), and I blend that into liquid. It makes a wonderful drink!

8. Drink eight to ten glasses of water a day. Make sure that the water you drink is pure. If you cannot filter your own water, buy it by the gallon from the grocery store. It's worth the money. There is simply no substitute.

9. Begin to move from processed foods to fresh foods. Understand that the more you cook or process your fresh fruits, vegetables, and grains, the more nutrients you lose. In her book *Food Smart!* Cheryl Townsley tells us that virtually no nutrients are lost in raw organic foods. However, you will lose 9 to 14 percent of the nutrients when you dry foods and 10 to 20 percent of the nutrients when you freeze them. Canning foods causes a loss of 35 to 50 percent of the nutrients.

10. Be consistent for at least four weeks. Habits that will last a lifetime can form that quickly. Your taste buds will change in about two weeks. Then you will start enjoying and craving fresh fruit, cooked or raw vegetables, nuts and whole grains, and lean protein.

11. Read other books about nutrition and diet. When I started my journey, I was so eager to learn, I read a few dozen books that helped me find a path that made sense to me. In appendix A, I've included a list of books that may help you find your path. (Many people have asked me about the food plan I use. I share it with you in chapter 18, where I answer frequently asked questions. But remember, you need to find the path that makes sense to you, and I know God will show you what that is.)

So now you have it. The bad list; the good list.

At this point several of you may be asking an important question: If it's that simple, why don't we just change the way we eat?

My first response to that question is that human nature is human nature. As I said in the beginning, people fail to make good choices about what they eat and how they relate to others because they lack either knowledge or willpower. At this point, I hope I've helped you gain a basic knowledge about which foods make poor choices and which make good choices. If you already have that understanding and still struggle, perhaps you lack willpower. And if that's the case, you may want to skip ahead to the steps to lasting change, part 6, which may very likely help you find the power to make lasting changes in both areas of struggle.

The truth is that we gravitate toward what is easy, convenient, and tasty rather than toward what is good. Robert Pritikin, son of the man who developed the Pritikin Diet Plan, makes one of my favorite statements about modern eating habits:

> Here is the dark irony of modern life that reveals just how powerful the fattening instinct is. Science has devoted millions of dollars to finding the diet most beneficial to human health. That diet has been discovered, yet no one wants to eat it.
>
> In fact, most of us do everything possible to avoid the diet we were designed to eat. The vast majority of Americans are no different from the Native Hawaiians, Australian Aborigines, or Pima Indians. When the Pima Indians were encouraged to go back to their traditional diets, they told the researchers, "No way." The same is true of the Australian Aborigines. In fact, one group of researchers actually offered to pay the Aborigines to eat their traditional diet in order to document its health effects. But after three months, the Aborigines flatly refused to continue, even for twice the money.
>
> On the surface, we all know why Americans, Pima Indians, Native Hawaiians, and Australian Aborigines would rather enjoy their high fat diets and be sick than eat the diet that would cure their diseases and give them good (overall) health.
>
> Simply put, the cure doesn't taste as good as the cause.[17]

Armed with the knowledge that foods affect our emotions—both positively and negatively—let's move on to the next section in the connection and see how our emotions then affect our relationships.

PART 3

OUR EMOTIONAL HEALTH AFFECTS OUR RELATIONSHIPS

CHAPTER SIX

When Food Threatens
Our Emotional Health

I n part 2 we talked about the foods that will affect our emotional states, for better or worse. Now it's time to take the connection between food and love to the next level. Let's examine the specific emotional changes that happen when we eat certain foods and how those emotions may affect our relationships. Some of the emotions that might be affected by our diet include feeling tired all the time, tired for no reason, restless, confused, easily frustrated, unexpectedly angry, impulsive, reactive, tearful, overwhelmed, and hopeless. Additionally we may experience a short attention span, craving for sweets, and low pain tolerance.[1]

You can imagine how these negative emotions would then affect our relationships. The following chart lists the specific emotions that have been directly linked to poor food choices. Let's take a look at each of these in detail and see how they affect the way we relate to others.

POSSIBLE WAYS FOOD AFFECTS OUR EMOTIONAL HEALTH	
POOR FOOD CHOICES	HEALTHY FOOD CHOICES
Poor self-image	Strong self-image
Isolation	Connection
Bad moods	Good moods
Irritability	Patience
Uncontrolled anger	Controlled anger
Mental confusion	Clear thinking
Depression	Joy

Each day, the food choices you make may be affecting your moods. Do you want to place yourself at risk for the negative emotions and moods that may result from poor food choices, or do you want to have the best opportunity for positive emotions and moods that result from good food choices?

POOR SELF-IMAGE OR STRONG SELF-IMAGE?

Self-image is a tricky thing. When I speak about self-image in relationship to food, I'm attempting to speak for the majority of people. There will always be someone who doesn't fit the typical pattern, someone whose body size is not affected by what he or she eats, or someone who truly doesn't mind being overweight.

That said, the typical pattern is this: As we eat a diet laden with poor foods such as those detailed in chapter 4, our self-image tends to be poor. Conversely, when we eat a diet made up of mostly the healthy foods listed in chapter 5, our self-image tends to be strong.[2]

The reason, I believe, is partly cultural.

In our culture being thin is good and being overweight is bad. Of course we know that this is definitely true from a physical health standpoint. But it is often also the case in our social circles. I've counseled hundreds of people who found it virtually impossible to secure a job at least in part because of their excess weight. And thousands of people suffering from excess weight have complained to me that they feel worthless in their relationships, unlovable, unable to extend or receive affection.

In addition, poor foods may lead to poor physical health. A person in poor health is much more likely to have a poor self-image, and the reasons why are obvious: An ill person will spend more time taking medications, feeling ill, seeing doctors, realizing limitations because of poor health. These, then, have an obvious affect on the way we see ourselves.

This part of the connection between love and food looks like this:

POOR FOODS ••• ▶ WEIGHT GAIN ••• ▶ POOR SELF-IMAGE

HEALTHY FOODS ••• ▶ NORMAL WEIGHT ••• ▶ STRONG SELF-IMAGE

A poor self-image affects our relationships in numerous ways. Primarily the problem is that the worse we feel about ourselves, the less likely we are to allow others to love us. We begin to feel we're not worthy of love, and at the same time we often become incapable of expressing love to others.

Likewise, when we feel positive about ourselves, we are more often open to receiving and giving love. Again many factors play a part in making our relationships work, but the connection between food and self-image as well as self-image and relationships is certainly one worth looking at. Especially if you struggle in either eating or relating and haven't been able to figure out a way to improve either.

My experience and the experiences of countless people I've counseled are that self-image is often the first emotional state that is affected by what we eat. The others tend to follow in what often becomes a pattern. Perhaps it's a pattern you recognize in yourself.

ISOLATION OR CONNECTION?

Our self-image is often directly involved in our ability to connect with others. I once counseled Jeff, who struggled with his food choices and his weight during the critical early teen years. As a junior high school student Jeff weighed more than two hundred pounds and was routinely teased. Because he was overweight and singled out for taunting, he had a very poor self-image and typically sat by himself during school meals. That didn't stop him from eating two fried burritos and two chocolate brownies every day at lunch.

The pattern I'm illustrating here was clearly evident in his life. Each day he made poor food choices, which contributed to his excess weight. His excess weight made him a target for negative social feedback, which, in turn, caused him to have a poor self-image. This, then, caused him to sit alone at lunch hour, aware that others were laughing at him and that none of them would want to be his friend.

Now there is evidence to back the fact that in people like Jeff, poor food choices may often lead to a poor self-image and eventually isolation.[3] The emotional states of poor self-image and isolation then led to weak and infrequent relationships among his peers. That, in turn, contributed to the fact that he was more often sick with bronchitis and other illnesses.

How did he pacify the pain in his life?

By eating more of the wrong foods. By loving himself with food.

I realize that Jeff's situation was somewhat extreme. Still, this dynamic is played out in the lives of more people than we might think. Perhaps it is played out in your life as well.

What happens when we become isolated? Obviously we are more alone, more closed in, less likely to share our feelings and hearts with those we love. We are also often a walking target for a host of other emotional states and conditions, some of them directly linked to specific types of processed and refined foods. Let's look at a few of those emotional states.

BAD MOODS OR GOOD MOODS?

Scientific research has proven that refined sugar and flour are responsible for changes in our moods or mood swings.[4] This is because refined sugar and flour cause changes in our blood sugar level. The moment we eat a food with these ingredients, our body reacts with a surge of blood sugar. How do we feel, and how does it look to other people? After eating the refined food product, we feel as if we are on a wonderful wave of energy and seem to be in a happy mood.

Ah, but the joyride never lasts.

Once a person's blood sugar begins to crash—and the world of medical science has long since known that this happens—the mood crash is almost always right behind it. The resulting sadness, frustration, and negativity is often chalked up to bad moods. People may conclude, "Oh, she always comes home from work in a bad mood." Or, "He has so much more anger at the children on the weekend."

People who say these things rarely take time to find out what their spouse or loved ones are eating before they come home from work or what weekend food consumption might be making Daddy's mood change from good to bad.

IRRITABILITY OR PATIENCE?

Not only do refined and processed foods play a role in whether we feel irritable or patient, but chemical additives can also leave us less able to cope with life's small inconveniences and unexpected twists.[5]

Joe was a man I counseled for a period of time. He frequently ate processed foods and additives such as sugar substitutes and caffeine. One afternoon a doctor told him his eating habits were taking a toll on his health. Joe had never been one to let a food or substance control him, and after hearing the doctor's advice, he quit all caffeine consumption virtually overnight, but he continued his poor eating habits.

He wasn't prepared for what came next.

In the absence of caffeine, Joe's patience became as thin as eggshells. Whereas it normally didn't bother him if his children played indoors and made a bit of noise, in the weeks after he eliminated caffeine, he found himself losing his temper almost hourly, yelling at the children for things that had never before been a problem. In addition, he began to be irritated by his wife, angered by habits she had had most of their married life and that had been a source of humor before his break with caffeine.

Finally, he asked his doctor about the change in his personality.

Caffeine, his doctor told him, had given him an artificial ability to cope with life.[6] Subconsciously this had led to greater caffeine intake and a greater dependence on it to survive the stress of life. Then, as excessive caffeine began to take its toll on Joe's physical and emotional health, he found himself caught between a physical rock and an emotional hard place.

Caffeine can affect your ability to cope. Rather than make sure you stop for an espresso in the morning, examine your life and see if you need to reduce your caffeine intake. If so, the good news is this: Once you've made the break from caffeine—or at least from heavy caffeine use—the symptoms of withdrawal that can leave you irritable will fade and eventually disappear.

Clearly the degree to which you are irritable or able to cope with life will affect your relationships. If you struggle with irritability in your relationships, consider including a small amount of protein at each meal or more whole grains, which are loaded with B vitamins. These vitamins tend to regulate blood sugar and stabilize moods.[7]

UNCONTROLLED ANGER OR CONTROLLED ANGER?

Bad moods and irritability are mild compared with bouts of uncontrolled anger. This type of emotional problem can be brought about because of a number of contributing factors. But let's say a person has made poor food choices for a significant period of time and as a result is overweight and suffering from a poor self-image. This, then, has led to mood swings and irritability.

Imagine that this pattern is left to grow unchecked in a person's emotional life for years. For some people in that situation, uncontrolled bouts of anger will soon follow.[8] Perhaps you know someone who flies off the handle easily or has unexplainable episodes of anger. Maybe it's you. If so, examine your situation and ask yourself what makes you so angry. Perhaps it's because you're trapped in a cycle that has left you feeling unfit and unloved.

Of course this is no excuse for moments of rage or uncontrolled anger.

But it might help illuminate the problem, and if the root of the problem is—at least in part—poor food choices, the time to make a change is now.

What happens to relationships when one of the people cannot control his or her anger? Far too often these relationships are destroyed in the process. In moments of extreme anger we tend to do and say things we wouldn't normally do or say. The hurt we can cause when operating from anger or rage is sometimes too great to repair without counseling and God's supernatural healing.

If you see yourself at this stage of poor emotional health, the time to act on your struggles and make a change is now. Remember, when you begin with a diet full of healthy foods, you will be more likely to feel good about yourself and in the process you may become more patient, less vulnerable to uncontrolled anger. You may even be open to professional counseling on anger management.

Again, many other factors can contribute to uncontrolled anger. But if a dietary change could help, just imagine how your relationships would benefit.

MENTAL CONFUSION OR CLEAR THINKING?

A diet high in sugar and processed foods has long been linked to mental confusion. Conversely, one anchored in healthy foods has been linked to sharper mental acuity or ability to think.[9] This is why children diagnosed with attention deficit disorder (ADD) or attention deficit hyperactivity disorder (ADHD) are first told to eliminate refined sugar, refined flour, and other processed, chemical-laden foods. Medication is never needed for many children once this dietary adjustment is made.

That being the case, how does mental confusion affect our relationships? In my counseling experience this emotional state seems to have a strong impact on a person's ability to get along with others. A relationship is a give-and-take in which one person expects the other person to listen and respond to the same degree he or she listens and responds.

Jeannie, a client of mine, struggled in her relationship with her children. Although she had the best intentions, when she saw the kids at the end of the day, she found herself consistently short-tempered and irritated with their childish behavior. She grew angry far too easily, and by the time she hit the pillow each night, she felt discouraged and defeated. "I love my kids," she told me. "But when we're together, I almost feel that I hate them."

Jeannie was worried her children would grow to resent her, remembering only the sad picture of their mother yelling at them or constantly berating them. As it turned out Jeannie was also dealing with a weight problem. Eating poor foods brought her a sense of comfort from her troubled relationships with her children. After learning that her diet might have something to do with her emotional health, Jeannie sought God's strength and changed her eating habits.

The change was remarkable.

She was gentle and calm, able to wade through the issues of homework, after-school sports, visits with friends, and sibling quarrels without coming undone. Later her oldest daughter said it this way: "Mom, I love you no matter what. But lately I know one hundred percent that you love me, too."

Jeannie told me this story in tears. "It's as if someone flipped on a switch in my brain, and suddenly I could hear everything I was saying. After getting rid of the junk in my diet—by God's strength, not my own—in two weeks the entire atmosphere in our home was improved."

And this may be true for you as well.

When husbands or wives find themselves being ignored or not heard by a spouse, arguments often follow. These can at times escalate to full-scale wars simply because one or both of them are suffering from mental confusion. Yes, factors other than food might cause a person to be mentally confused or unable to think clearly, but certainly it is worth examining one's diet to see if maybe foods have played a role in leading to an emotional state that has hurt your relationships.

DEPRESSION OR JOY?

Depression is a term that is thrown around loosely these days, so I want to make one thing clear up front. Many people suffer from clinical depression for a host of reasons—none of which may have anything to do with food. Clinically depressed people may have thoughts of suicide or severe sorrow. They may act irrationally and become very forgetful. At times their thoughts border on being obsessive and extreme. If these characteristics apply to you, my suggestion is that you seek immediate help by seeing a professional counselor.

If you are such a person, this section may apply to you, or it may not. For the most part it applies to the person who is in the early stages of depression, the emotional state when the blues seem almost impossible to shake off. These people may feel discouraged or defeated. They are still functioning but not in the joyful life they know is possible.

What I've found in counseling is that there is a cycle of sorts when one or more people in a relationship are feeling depressed. The more depressed a person feels, the more harm this emotional state does to relationships. The more harm it does to relationships, the more depressed the person becomes.

It seems to me that depression is what happens when many of the previous emotional states have already been reached. Once a person has a poor self-image and has given way to a lifestyle of isolation (even within a relationship), once the person has fallen prey to poor moods and irritability, pessimism or uncontrolled anger, mental confusion or anxiety, then feelings of depression are generally not far behind.

In addition, the brain's reaction to refined and processed foods has been proven to be linked to feelings of depression.[10]

I once counseled George, whose wife had slipped into this routine. In the beginning of their marriage both George and his wife were happily in love and feeling very good about themselves and the love they shared. But after two years at a desk job, George's wife began to find comfort in eating wrong foods. This in turn kicked off a cycle much like the one we just discussed, and in the end his wife was caught sinking in the miry mud of depression.

For weeks and weeks George did his best to come home from work with enough happiness for both of them. He would question her about her day, smile as much as possible, and look for ways to make her feel loved. But when this didn't seem to be improving his wife's condition, George began shutting down. It wasn't long before he began confiding in a woman at work, someone who had noticed the concern in his eyes, the way he wasn't as lighthearted as before.

By the time I saw George, he was on the verge of having an affair.

Did he blame his wife's depression? No, he blamed himself. But the fact remained that he felt helpless to pull her out of the rut she had fallen into.

The question is this: What should you do if you or someone you love has slipped into a depression? Seek professional help, especially if you have any concerns that the depression is chemical in nature or clinical. But even if you get professional help, take a hard look at the foods you eat. Perhaps the connection between food and love is playing a part in making you feel depressed.

Dad's Too Tired to Play

When my son Michael was young, I ate a typical American high-fat, overly processed diet. Even though I was exercising, I was still very tired. I remember Michael's asking me to play football with him, and I would play for a little while. But then I would be exhausted. He would get upset and tell me that he was going to have his kids while he was young so that by the time he was my age (forty-five at the time), his kids would be grown and out of the house.

He wanted me to play with him more, and he recognized that I was too tired and listless to be much fun, even though he didn't understand the reasons why. It makes me sad today, now that I understand the connection between how we eat and how we love.

I can't go back and undo the past, and neither can you. But I can make healthy choices for the future. That way when my grandkids run up and want to play, I will find myself romping about like a child, full of vigor and boundless energy.

Think about your life and your energy level. If you find yourself crawling out of bed in the morning and falling asleep at nine o'clock at night exhausted, there's a very good chance it's because of the way you eat.

The point is this: Foods may be affecting our moods and energy levels, and that in turn affects our relationships. That was certainly the case for me.

If you knew you could change your eating habits and gain a better level of physical and emotional health in the process, wouldn't you at least give it a try? I'm sure most of you would say yes. But many of you would also say, "We've tried that, and we've always failed. We simply can't eat the right foods."

Keep reading. I believe that with God's strength you can, indeed, make these changes. Some practical help about how to tap into that strength is up ahead at the end of this book.

CHAPTER SEVEN

How Poor Emotional Health Can Affect Marriage

L et's get specific. As many of you know, I travel around the country giving seminars primarily on marriage relationships. When God began showing me that what we eat has a direct impact on our emotions, that our emotions directly affect our relationships, and that our relationships have a direct impact on our health, I got an idea.

Why not survey the thousands of married people who attend my seminars?

The survey results were incredibly revealing. I believe you'll see yourself in some of their comments. This information told me that there was a direct link between eating poorly and loving poorly. In addition, there was a strong connection between healthy eating and healthy loving, one that for many people isn't possible without the information revealed in the last section of this book.

The emotions we discussed in the last chapter lead to certain common issues, which I'll call symptoms of a failing marriage. They include indifference and withdrawal, irritability and anxiety, low self-esteem and depression. Now let's see how these symptoms can tear at what may be your most vital relationship.

INDIFFERENCE AND WITHDRAWAL

People who turn to processed foods for comfort, entertainment, and companionship often turn away from the people they love. It can get to the point that in their quest for food rewards, these people often ignore their spouses. In reality, the food rewards are destroying not only their health but also their marriages. Similarly, the spouse of someone who makes poor food choices can also suffer from indifference, wondering whether the relationship is worth the effort it takes to maintain it.

Many people in my seminars found that their poor food choices led to indifference and withdrawal in their relationships. Read the following excerpts, and imagine the pain and hopelessness behind every word. Maybe you will see yourself in these responses.

- My family has been critical of my weight gain, which started after my wife and I got married. I have tried to lose it several times, but I have not been successful. I think it's a control issue, even though my wife says it doesn't matter to her. I feel myself losing interest in my marriage. I can see it in her eyes.
- Food has affected my marriage negatively. I have gained weight, and as a result, my self-esteem has been affected, and I have been sexually cold.
- I am an overeater, as a result I am about forty pounds over my target body weight. I don't feel very good about my own body, and my husband is embarrassed by my appearance. He is very patient and encouraging, but I know he is less affectionate to me because of it.
- When I have gained weight, it makes me feel less attractive, which affects my desire for complete intimacy.
- I went through a time when I ate too much and gained weight. Fat is not good for a marriage.
- My eating habits have caused me to gain sixty pounds during our marriage, and that bugs my wife. She loves me but would love to have the old me back. I can feel myself drifting away from her.
- My compulsive eating has caused me to lie to my spouse about where I have been and what I have done. We are losing trust in each other.
- My husband and I went through a dry spell for a while, and I found more enjoyment in a candy bar than I did in him. This made me feel worse because I have gained weight I cannot lose.
- My husband believes food is just to sustain life and energy. For me, food is more emotional and social; thus mealtime can be challenging in our home.
- I have a hard time controlling my weight because my wife constantly brings bad foods into the house. This causes stress between us, and I don't look forward to mealtimes anymore.

Did you see yourself at all? Did you see your spouse? Maybe this is the first time you realized that bad food choices may be a cause of some problems you are having in your marriage.

If that is the case, don't lose heart. There is hope for you. Lots of hope.

Dan would tell you that, too. Several years ago he had no clue how his eating habits put his marriage into danger.

The moment of truth for Dan came the afternoon his wife, Sue, met him at the restaurant where he worked as general manager. Her face was pained, and there were tears in her eyes as she asked him to sit down.

"Dan, I'm at the end of my rope about our marriage," she said. "You've got to do something about your health, or I'm not sure I can stay with you. In fact, I have found someone else."

Dan felt as if a club had hit him in the chest. While he was stunned at the reality of Sue's ultimatum, he was not surprised that she was confronting him. He immediately knew what she was talking about when she mentioned his health. He knew he had an eating problem. But he didn't know it would lead to this.

As he tried to find words to say to his wife, he bit his lip and looked out the window. How had he allowed this to happen?

He had been very athletic as a child, running and moving and jumping almost constantly. At the same time he developed a hearty appetite. He could eat three bowls of cereal for breakfast, snack between meals, eat two sandwiches for lunch, and still have room for a double serving of dinner and dessert before bed.

That carried over into his high school and college years, when he was active in football, soccer, and track. But when he married Sue and took a job managing a five-star restaurant, his active lifestyle changed dramatically. His eating habits changed, too.

They got worse.

The absence of physical activity in Dan's life left a void he needed to fill. Instead of taking up tennis with Sue or jogging with her, he passed the time eating. At the restaurant where he worked, food was always available, and every day brought about a different culinary creation, a different way to pacify the loss.

It had taken several months before Sue had noticed a change in Dan's appearance. "Are you gaining weight?" she had asked him bluntly one afternoon. "Your stomach looks as if it's breaking through your shirt buttons."

In all his life, Dan had never felt the feelings that coursed through him in that moment. Because of his athletic involvement, he had been accepted by the guys and sought after by the girls as far back as he could remember.

But Sue's disgusted tone told him clearly that, at least in her eyes, his worth was directly linked to his looks.

Whether or not she intended to, Sue seemed more distant after their conversation that day. A few days later when Dan was getting undressed for bed, he caught her staring at his midsection. Suddenly he felt the way Adam and Eve must have felt when they realized they were naked—ashamed and anxious to cover up.

These concerns led Dan to promise to stop eating certain foods and to lose some weight. But the more he thought about giving up sugar and fat, the more they seemed to call his name. A year later he knew he was addicted. The only time he felt happiness and comfort—the feelings he used to have with Sue—was when he was eating the foods he knew he shouldn't eat. Psychiatrist Gerald May says in his book *Addiction and Grace* that all addictions are medications for weak relationships. That was true for Dan.

As his eating and exercise habits continued to decline, so did his intimacy with Sue.

Now he sat across the table from his wife, hearing the words every husband dreads: "I have found someone else."

"I don't want to lose you," Dan told his wife. Tears streamed down her face, and the agony in her eyes tore at Dan's heart. "Would you really leave me?"

She reached out and touched his cheek, as if longing for something they hadn't shared in years. "Dan, if something doesn't change, I'm afraid it's my only way out."

"Please, Sue, give me another chance. I'll do whatever it takes."

What it took for Dan and Sue was an honest look at how issues about food had driven a wedge in their marriage. After talking and praying about their situation with some trusted friends, Dan confessed his obsession with food and asked Sue to forgive him for allowing it to threaten their marriage. Sue confessed her withdrawal and her allowing herself to become attracted to another man.

They knew they didn't have strength to solve their problems on their own, and they looked to God's grace and power to help them rebuild their marriage and to change Dan's unhealthy eating patterns.

Dan and Sue were willing to get help by following the same principles you'll read in the last section of this book. At first Dan was as confused as I was about how to cry out for God's help. It's really no different from the millions who have cried out to God within Alcoholics Anonymous. The difference for me now is that I understand accessing God's power a little better than I ever did before. No matter how long it may take, you also will find strength from God to overcome the eating patterns that may be contributing to the indifference and withdrawal in your marriage.

IRRITABILITY AND ANXIETY

Did you know that unhealthy eating can lead to irritability and anxiety, two dynamics that are very trying on a marriage? Someone with a short fuse is often suffering from irritability. This reaction, which causes people to feel nervous and anxious, is the cause of many troubled marriages. But is it really the cause? The research I've used in putting together this book clearly shows that at least one cause of irritability is poor eating habits. As you're about to see, irritability does not lead to peaceful intimacy in a marriage. The same thing is true with people who are anxious much of the time.

The sad fact is that our diets often leave us too irritable and anxious to love or laugh with or play with our spouses.[1] Here's what a few of the people at my seminars have told me about the way poor food choices have affected them:

- I eat the wrong foods, and my low energy and stamina make me feel tired and crabby.
- My wife and I often eat the wrong things—fat, sugar—thus lowering our energy and self-esteem. We don't look as good as we did, we wait too long to eat, we make poor decisions, and we have shorter tempers.
- Sugar makes me agitated toward my spouse during certain parts of my cycle.
- If my wife and I eat sugar and caffeine, we have less patience and tolerance for each other and our kids.
- Since we have been dating, we are exercising less and gaining lots of weight. We're not happy about that, and we end up being grouchy with each other.
- I don't cook nutritious meals because I don't have the time. My weight has ballooned, and my energy is sapped. I often feel short-tempered with my husband and family.
- I find that if I eat foods with sugar, my hands get shaky and I feel anxious about so many things.

Again, did you see yourself? Did you see your spouse? Are you beginning to see the connection between your food choices and your relationships?

Carrie finally did, and it changed her life.

It was three o'clock in the morning one January, and Carrie lay trembling under the covers next to her sleeping husband. Her heart had slipped into an unrecognizable rhythm, first racing, then fluttering, then missing beats and pounding out an erratic pattern against her chest wall.

I'm going to die, she thought. Her throat felt thick and dry, and she swallowed hard. Was her throat closing up on her? She swallowed again and felt a wave of nausea building deep in her gut. A dozen options flitted through her mind. Should she call 9-1-1? Get up and take a hot bath to calm her nerves? Run to the bathroom and make herself throw up?

"Help me, Lord . . . ," she whispered into the night.

Her husband, Dennis, rolled over and placed his arm across her midsection. Moving his face closer to hers, he tried to find her lips in the darkness, but Carrie pulled away.

"Not tonight . . . I'm feeling sick." Her heart fluttered for several seconds, her body stiff and unyielding.

Turning back onto his other side, her husband let out a disgusted sigh. "When are you going to do something about yourself?"

Suddenly tears filled her eyes. She could sense his irritation. He was right. It was a disgusting situation. She began to wonder if *she* was disgusting. Her body had grown from a size 8 to a size 16 in a year. *What is happening to me? What is happening to our marriage?* she wondered.

The attacks were so frightening, so physically draining that they often kept her from having a physical relationship with her husband. The days that followed usually found her wracked with exhaustion and unable to play tennis or take walks with Dennis—something that had been a hallmark of their earlier married days.

She buried her face, speaking softly into the pillowcase, "I need help."

Shortly after that night, Carrie did find help. She learned that the frightening sensations she was experiencing were the result of anxiety, which took the form of frequent panic attacks. And Carrie also learned that one of the factors that led to her anxiety and irritability was her body's physical response to excess sugar.

Sugar. That began to make sense to her. She did eat lots of sugary foods, foods high in processed carbohydrates. And because those foods had never satisfied her appetite, she ate even more of them. So both her weight gain and anxiety could be traced, in part, to sugar.

After doing some reading, Carrie found out that sugar can be one of the deadliest nonfoods in existence.[2] She began to understand the connection between what she ate, how she loved, and the truth that only in God's strength could she find the ability to change.

Today she is a new person, quite literally. She eats mostly healthy, wholesome foods and has energy for all the things she enjoys doing—both during the day and night. In addition, she's lost sixty pounds. She and Dennis are more in love than ever before. And Dennis still is in grateful shock.

LOW SELF-ESTEEM AND DEPRESSION

Have you ever eaten three doughnuts in one sitting or a triple-scoop ice cream sundae and then felt your mind grow suddenly foggy? Research from several nutrition experts suggests that many people are affected this way by refined foods such as white sugar and white flour.[3] As the mind grows foggy, it is common for these same people to feel negative about themselves or to become depressed. Typically these symptoms are linked to feelings of guilt and shame that come as a result of eating wrong foods. Other symptoms are merely the emotional response to that foggy feeling.

Either way, the resulting range of emotions can greatly affect the marriage relationship. Take a look at what some of the people I surveyed had to say about how poor food choices gave them feelings of low self-esteem and depression.

- The vicious cycle of depression, overeating, and low self-esteem affected how I felt, how I viewed myself physically. Then I transferred those views onto my impression of how my wife must feel about me.
- For me, overeating = low self-esteem = depression.
- The healthier I eat, the better I feel about myself. As a result, I am able to feel better about my relationships and can give more.
- Lack of discipline proved to be very costly. When I gained weight, my husband was less interested in physical intimacy. I found myself physically unattractive, and so did he.
- I feel fat and undesirable. I can't believe I have no self-control. I used to criticize overweight people before, saying that if they really wanted to lose weight, they could.

- Bad eating habits caused us to gain about thirty to fifty pounds each. We've been married six years, and we have less self-esteem, less confidence, less physical attraction, and naturally less sexual intimacy.
- Overeating in our relationship has lead to being overweight. This has added stress to our marriage due to heightened feelings of insecurity and lower self-confidence.
- I eat too many sweets, which makes me overweight. This makes me unhappy with how I look, and my wife is no longer proud of me.
- I am an emotional eater; it is an escape for me. I will sometimes drown my troubles in food instead of working through them.
- I think my eating habits have lowered my self-esteem. I have gained a hundred pounds since I got married. I do not like to see myself undressed, so I know my husband is disgusted by my appearance, even though it has not lowered his desire for sex.

If you saw yourself in the list of responses, don't be discouraged. Bill's story illustrates the hope that can be yours.

Bill's days were always busy. As an attorney for a powerful law firm, courtroom appearances took up most mornings, and he was often too busy to eat lunch. Client meetings tended to start in the early afternoon, and sometimes it was four o'clock when he finally organized his notes from the day and realized that he was hungry.

Bill's solution? Five bags of potato chips from the lunchroom vending machine. They were easy to eat, tasted good, and seemed to give him the energy he needed to get through the afternoon and home to his apartment near downtown Chicago.

In time Bill gained forty pounds and could no longer fit into his suits. Money was tight, and his wife, Darla, was not happy about Bill's physical appearance. In an attempt to mind their money well and to give himself the incentive to lose weight, Bill began dressing for work more casually than before. Once his boss joked that Bill looked more like a bum off the street than a businessman.

Although Bill tried a dozen diets, he was unable to lose weight, and after two years he felt terrible about himself. What did he do to make himself feel better? Hit the vending machine and eat more potato chips and other refined snack foods.

"You don't seem happy," his wife would tell him when he got home each day.

"I'm fine," he would manage, without making eye contact. "I'd feel better if I had new clothes."

"You'd feel better if you lost weight. You'd look better, too."

This exchange wasn't the same every night, obviously, but it was similar enough that at the end of that year they wound up in marriage counseling. When nothing seemed to help, they wondered if their marriage would survive. That's when they attended one of my seminars. There they heard me talk about the connection between food and love, and suddenly a light went on for both of them.

Could it be that food was playing a role in Bill's low self-esteem and depression?

Darla decided to let Bill come to his own conclusions, and the week after attending my seminar, he made some significant changes. He realized that his body needed fuel at certain intervals, and he took time to eat a nutritious lunch. Then he did what most people can't. He fasted from junk food for one month. He gave up his chips and ate an apple or some cheese if he got hungry in the late afternoon. Then he would come home for dinner and eat the salad, vegetables, and lean meat his wife would prepare.

What he and Darla discovered was absolutely amazing. He began to feel better about himself, and over a period of months he lost weight. Eventually he fit into his nice suits again. In the process he began coming home happier and ready to involve himself in the interaction of his marriage. Over time, they watched their relationship grow.

The effects were so astounding that Bill made a decision to stop eating refined food products for one year. He admitted that without God's strength that decision would have been impossible to carry out. He implemented some of the specific tools detailed in part 6 of this book, and his life began to change permanently. That was three years ago, and today his relationship with Darla is sound and satisfying. Every now and then they'll eat junk foods on holidays or other special events, but the pull those foods once had and the way they contributed to Bill's poor emotional health is gone from their lives for good.

In its place is the relationship they once feared they would never have.

BEAUTY FROM ASHES

I hope that you're encouraged by what you have just read. Even if you are in worse shape than Dan or Carrie or Bill, I know that God can take your situation and bring beauty out of the ashes. He's done it for them, and he will do it for you. It's never too late.

Regardless of past failures, you can have complete health! The principles in this book will help you have the healthy marriage and body you've always dreamed of. Why? Because you will have a new understanding about how food affects your relationships, and you will learn that God's strength will help you make the changes. God wants you to have a healthy body and healthy relationships. He knows that if you eat right, you will have:

- More time to enjoy the life and ministry he has for you because you will be sick less often.
- More emotional stability. Healthy food helps us feel upbeat and energized; unhealthy food leaves us in the same situation as the people we've discussed in this chapter.
- More mental alertness. Good food reduces brain fog and helps our memory.
- More physical energy. Eating the right foods and doing moderate exercise allows you to lose the weight you want and feel great with less stiffness or soreness. Exercise gives back more energy than you use.
- More relaxed nights with great sleep.
- More money in your pocket. The healthier you are—physically and emotionally—the less money you will need to spend on medicines and doctors.

Now that you understand how food affects our relationships, in part 4 we'll take a closer look at the one thing that can harm our physical health more than a diet of refined, processed foods: damaged relationships.

The next stage of the vicious cycle involving food and love involves the way our relationships can literally affect our physical health. And poor physical health often leaves many people attempting to comfort themselves with food and other cheap substitutes.

The quality of our relationships is a key to this cycle. Particularly the marriage relationship.

The fact is that we're created for interaction both with God and others, and when that interaction is missing in our lives, we tend to fill the void with substitutes—a primary filler being poor foods.

Remember, we're talking about making changes that will affect your relationships and physical health for a lifetime. I hope you're as excited as I am!

I truly believe if we follow the steps laid out in the pages ahead, we will affect not only our marriages and families but also the entire country in the process. My dream is that as people apply these truths, they will have healthier marriages, healthier bodies, and less need to use food as a substitute for love. Ultimately I hope to see a decrease in the need to spend billions of dollars in medical costs each year as we break into a period of God-designed health.

Read on!

PART 4

OUR RELATIONSHIPS
AFFECT OUR PHYSICAL
HEALTH

CHAPTER EIGHT

Poor Relationships
Lead to Poor Health

T here once was a small boy who played Little League. He wasn't as talented as the other nine-year-olds on the team, but his father adored him and made sure he always sat in the stands, cheering his son's team on to victory. Week after week the coach was surprised to see the father because the man's son never started a game. In fact, the boy spent more time on the bench than on the field.

Toward the end of the season, the boy came to a game by himself for the first time. "Coach," he said, tracing the toe of his shoe in the dirt and squirming anxiously. "Would it be okay if I started today?"

The coach considered the boy's request and decided it wouldn't hurt. The team had already locked up a position in the playoffs. What harm could it possibly cause to start the boy that afternoon?

"Okay, but do your best." He was about to ask the boy why his father wasn't there, but something made him change his mind. "Now get out there, and warm up."

The boy raced out to join his teammates, and that day he played the game of his life. He was three-for-four with a home run and a double, and he made two plays that launched his team to victory. When the contest was over, the coach hugged the boy and tapped the bill of his cap. "That's the best you've ever played. What in the world came over you today?"

The boy grinned, and his eyes grew wet. "Well, Coach, it was a special day for me." He hesitated, and a single tear rolled down his cheek. "You see, my father was blind, and he was very sick." The boy hung his head, and a sob escaped. But just as quickly the smile returned, and he met the coach's gaze once more. "He died last week. And today . . . well, sir, today he's in heaven. So even though he never missed any of my games, this was the first one he got to see."

This modern-day folktale has been told again and again, but only recently did I realize how much like the boy's father I had been. There I was, in the middle of the marriage game for the past several decades, but all the while I was blind to an aspect of relationships that affects us at a very deep level.

For years I've joined the voices of experts telling couples how to make love last, how to love better, and how to deepen their marriages. I've written books about communication, conflict resolution, commitment, sex, religion, and a dozen other topics. But I had completely missed the idea that food affects our relationships, that relationships affect our health, and that people often fill the void of poor relationships with poor food, condemning themselves to a terribly destructive cycle.

Now that I can finally see the importance of this connection, let me show you some examples of what I've learned.

KEEP THE CONNECTION IN MIND

As you read the next chapters, keep in mind the parts of the cycle we've already discussed: the connection between food and emotions and relationships. My goal in this part of the book is to discuss the next step in the cycle: how our relationships affect our health and how you can improve your relational skills. If our poor eating habits have affected our emotions and our poor emotional health has affected our relationships, then it's time to see what happens next.

Think about this, too: For some of you, weak relationships and poor health may be your entry point into the destructive cycle. Maybe your entry point was not poor food choices; at least that may not have been your initial problem. Maybe you never had trouble with your eating habits until you began struggling in your relationships. Poor relationships then led to poor overall health (emotionally and physically), and this may have led you to fill the holes in your life with cheap substitutes, which for many people mean bad food choices. I'll discuss that at length in later chapters.

Either way, keep the connection in mind as you read this section, and realize that any discussion about relationships is designed to fit this part of the food-love connection and the cycle that can result.

THE WAY WE LOVE AFFECTS OUR HEALTH

The essence of this book is how poor food choices can contribute to poor relationships, how poor relationships can contribute to poor health, and how the result leaves us with holes that we often fill with poor foods, thus creating a cycle. Now, though, we'll take a closer look at how our relationships, especially our marriages, affect our health and immune systems.

Here is the key: The better we eat, the better our emotional health will be. The stronger our emotional health, the stronger our relationships can be, with more energy and better moods. These strong relationships allow us to love deeply. The deeper we love, the more trusting, open, honest, and satisfying our relationships are. The more satisfying our relationships, the greater chance we'll have for good physical health, and in many cases the less likely we'll be to get a major disease.

The more attention we pay to healthy eating and lifestyle habits, the more focused and open we will likely be to loving the way God intended us to love. And healthy, loving relationships make us physically healthier.

EVIDENCE FROM RESEARCH

Several research studies have demonstrated the impact that loving, caring relationships have on physical health. Let me share just a few of those with you here.

The Rabbit Study

One interesting study involved rabbits. Scientists put groups of rabbits in cages, fed them high-cholesterol foods for several months, and then tested them.[1] For the most part, the results were not very surprising. Because of their poor diet, the rabbits had greatly elevated cholesterol in their veins and arteries.

All of them but the ones in the lower cage.

Why, the researchers wondered, would only these rabbits not be affected by the poor diet? The researchers checked further and found that one of the female lab attendants had taken a liking to the rabbits in this cage. Every day, after recording research information about the rabbits, she would give them some personal attention, taking them out of the cage, snuggling with them, petting them, and playing with them.

She did this every day.

The researchers thought this was fascinating and decided to implement the "love" variable on a broader scale. This time they put three groups of rabbits in three separate cages and fed them fatty foods. Every day they took the A group out of their cage and played with them for a period of time, hugging them, snuggling them close, and petting them. The B group they touched only once in a while, and the C group they never touched at all.

When the experiment was over and the researchers tested all three groups, they found that the C group had a high buildup of cholesterol, the B group had a little less buildup, and—not surprisingly—the A group had significantly less cholesterol buildup. The only variable was how much attention and loving care the rabbits in the groups received.

One basic truth seemed to emerge from the research: Although the rabbits ate the same unhealthy food, those that were given attention and love developed more effective ways to handle the bad food they were eating. In other words, there was a significant link between healthy love and physical health.

The Love-and-Ulcer Study

The *American Journal of Epidemiology* reported another study that reveals the correlation between love and physical health.[2] For a five-year period a university research project studied 8,500 men who had no previous history or symptoms of ulcers. By the end of the study, 250 of the men developed ulcers. What was the variable?

In the questionnaire that the men filled out at the beginning of the study, they had to answer questions about their relationships, including questions about their marriages. One of the study's findings was that the men who reported a low level of love from their wives were more than twice as likely to have ulcers as the men who reported a high level of love from their wives.

Furthermore, the men who indicated that their wives did not love them were almost three times as likely to have ulcers as those whose wives showed their love and support on a daily basis.

The Alameda Isolation Study

An Alameda, California, study concluded that people who were isolated from meaningful relationships had a greater risk of death. In 1965, Dr. Berkman and her colleagues at the California Department of Health Services studied nearly 7,000 men and women living in Alameda County, located near San Francisco. Nine years into the study, the researchers found that people who lacked social and community ties—who were not married, who had little contact with family and friends, and who were not members of churches or other groups—were two to three times more likely to die than the people who had healthy relationships.[3]

"This association between social and community ties and premature death was found to be independent of and a more powerful predictor of health and longevity than age, gender, race, socioecomonic status, self-reported physical health status, and health practices such as smoking, alcoholic beverage consumption, overeating, physical activity, and utilization of preventive health services as well as a cumulative index of health practices. Those who lacked social ties were at increased risk of dying from coronary heart disease, stroke, cancer, respiratory diseases, gastrointestinal diseases, and all other causes of death."[4]

The Forgiveness-and-Illness Studies

Several studies have been conducted to prove there is a connection between a person's ability to forgive and his or her physical health. These studies found that the moral structure of a person—his or her ability to forgive and to live by the Golden Rule—made a dramatic impact on both the chances of contracting an illness and the body's ability to fight back.

The studies showed that many times when the negative feelings of unforgiveness are carried around in the body, they begin to act on a person's immune system.[5]

This is also true if the person you need to forgive is yourself.

The Cold-and-Love Study

The *Journal of the American Medical Association* reported a study that dealt with the common cold and other everyday illnesses. Researchers found stronger immune systems in people with different types of satisfying relationships. In one study, people were intentionally infected with the cold virus. Participants who had meaningful relationships with numerous people did not develop a cold as often as those who did not have such relationships.[6]

By the way, after changing my diet and really focusing on my relationships, I haven't had a cold or any illness in almost two years.

The truth from this study seemed to be that social support in all areas of a person's life is invaluable to the health of the immune system. Therefore love truly does seem to be the key to health.

The Hostility Factor

Dean Ornish, author of *Love and Survival,* cites forty-five studies in which the combined research points to an astounding connection between hostility and coronary heart disease. In each study, hostility proved to be one of the most important variables in this type of heart condition.

He says, "The affects of hostility are equal or greater in magnitude to the traditional factors for heart disease, elevated cholesterol level, high blood pressure, etc. I believe hostility is a manifestation of a more fundamental issue, loneliness and isolation. People who feel lonely and isolated are often angry and hostile. When they act with chronic anger they tend to drive people away, causing them to feel even more lonely and isolated in a vicious cycle."[7]

You can see how the relationship of an irritated and critical husband or wife can cause internal hostility and put distance in a marriage. This, then, will increase the hostile person's chances of suffering a major disease.

STEP BACK

The implications of these studies are profound. The quality of your relationships directly affects your health. Isn't that amazing?

Think about the implications for your own life. Do you have relationships in which you regularly give and receive love? If not, your health may be at risk.

What are you willing to do to change that?

As I began to understand the connection between food and love, I read studies that lent tremendous scientific support to what I was seeing. If food has contributed to a weakened relationship, then that weakened relationship may contribute to weakened physical health. This research appeared in a number of books I read, but Dean Ornish's perspective in *Love and Survival* captured my attention. Listen to what Dr. Ornish says in summarizing this connection: "When you feel loved and nurtured, cared for, supported and intimate, you are much more likely to be happier and healthier. You have a much lower risk of getting sick, and if you do, you have a much greater chance of survival." He continues, "The researchers found that feelings of being loved and emotionally supported were more important predictors of the severity of coronary artery blockages than the number of relationships a person had. Equally important, this effect is independent of diet, smoking, exercise, cholesterol, family history, genetics, and other standard risk factors."[8]

Ornish reaches several conclusions in the course of his research:

- The health of people who have intimate, close, caring relationships with family, friends, neighbors, loved ones is drastically better than those who don't.

- The health of people who have emotional and verbal support (friends or neighbors who will be available in times of need) is drastically better than those who don't.
- The health of people who have the opportunity for intimacy is greatly superior than those who don't.
- People who actively give and receive love from other people are three to five times less likely to contract serious or fatal health problems. These diseases include increased risk of heart attack, stroke, infectious diseases, many types of cancer, allergies, arthritis, tuberculosis, autoimmune diseases, low birth rate, low Apgar scores, alcoholism, drug abuse, suicide, and so on.
- The quality of your relationships—how loving and supportive they are—is more important than the number of those relationships.[9]

MY FATHER'S SAD LEGACY

When I recently celebrated my sixtieth birthday, I realized I'm the first Smalley male who has not had a heart attack in his fifties. I began to wonder if perhaps the deaths of my father and brother weren't somehow linked to the way they related to people. The way they loved.

As I pored over some of the research studies I've cited in this chapter, I thought more deeply about my father and brother and their early deaths. I believe now that a lifetime of poor food choices contributed to their poor emotional health, and that, in turn, affected the way they related to people. And those very relationships almost certainly played a role in their early deaths.

There is nothing healthy about living in a strained marriage, a marriage where both people are not loving and serving each other the way Christ loved and served the church. My father's life was a perfect illustration of this.

Dad was an angry man. He was very isolated. I never once saw my dad hug my mom, and I don't ever remember his hugging me. He wouldn't sleep in the same room with my mother, or she wouldn't sleep with him because he snored too loud. He probably had sleep apnea—something I also have.

I do not know for sure what foods might have led to my father's poor emotional health, but clearly his food choices had led to excessive weight, and that, in turn, definitely played a role in the way he lived, loved, and died.

Remember the emotional conditions we've already discussed—isolation, poor self-image, irritability. These were all factors in Dad's emotional makeup. By the time I was old enough to observe the relationship he and my mother shared, Dad slept in a garage bedroom by himself.

The closest I got to touching him was when I would lie on his arm in his garage bedroom, where we would listen to baseball games on the radio together. I would rest my face on his arm, the feel of his rough skin beneath my young cheek, and I would blow out the match when he lit a cigarette. One cigarette after another.

That's the most meaningful thing I can remember in my relationship with my dad. He was a man who had never learned about healthy eating or its affect on healthy loving. He had never learned the importance of communicating with my mom or the benefits of oneness in a marriage and the bonding of physical touch. It makes sense to me now why my dad died of a heart attack at an early age.

The same thing was true with my brother Ronnie, who was four years older than I and who died of a heart attack when he was fifty-one. He was a very angry person who distrusted doctors. He lived on the same refined and processed diet many Americans exist on, and that diet led to the blocked arteries that eventually took his life.

When I think about Ronnie, I think of the correlation Dean Ornish made between hostility and heart disease. Ronnie was irritated at the slightest thing that went wrong and was closed and limited in his commitments. He was hostile, isolated, fearful, and distrusting, and research proves that this harmed his relationships, which, in turn, may likely have had a direct impact on his heart trouble.[10]

Now that I reflect on my father and brother, I am saddened to see how the impact of their food choices and their weak relationships affected their health. It makes me even more committed to share with others what I have discovered about food and love.

I hope that the information in this chapter will nudge you to reflect on your own life and the lives of the people close to you. How is your health affected by relationships that are loving or that lack love? How does your own love or lack of love affect the health of the people around you?

The next chapter will share some very practical principles for strengthening your love—and your health.

CHAPTER NINE

Love As the Key to Health

T he research about love and health reveals an interesting truth: People are more likely to choose life-enhancing behaviors rather than self-destructive ones when they feel loved and cared for. And when they love someone else.[1]

In other words, it is not only how much love you get but also how much you give. Both giving and receiving love have a healing effect. And both the giver and the receiver benefit.

WE ARE CREATED FOR RELATIONSHIP

My favorite definition of real love is a love that is more concerned about others than it is about itself. The very highest form of love is defined in the New Testament: "Don't be selfish; don't live to make a good impression on others. Be humble, thinking of others as better than yourself. Don't think only about your own affairs, but be interested in others, too, and what they are doing. Your attitude should be the same that Christ Jesus had."[2]

First and foremost, God has created us with the relational need to connect with him in meaningful and satisfying ways. His ultimate will, as stated by Christ, is that we are to love him with all our heart, soul, and mind, and to love our neighbor as we love ourselves.[3] These two actions—loving God and loving our neighbor as we love ourselves—are the healthiest way to live, according to the Bible and according to current research.

If we love well, we're less likely to have holes in our hearts from being unfulfilled. A satisfied heart has less reason to turn to unhealthy foods for emotional fulfillment. Therefore, healthy love leads to good health for many reasons.

If, on the other hand, we disconnect from God in a meaningful relationship and/or disconnect or develop weak relationships with people, then our health is greatly affected in a negative way. Here are some truths that explain what happens to our bodies when we do not have the healthy relationships God created us for.

- We are more likely to turn to unhealthy foods to fill the holes in our hearts.
- We are more likely to get caught in the terrible cycle of destruction that can exist between food and love.
- We are more likely to have a weakened immune system.
- We are more susceptible to illness and disease.
- We greatly increase our chances of developing a life-threatening or fatal disease such as cancer, diabetes, and heart disease.
- Our bodies do not function smoothly. All systems tend to work ineffectively.
- We are more apt to have chronic physical and mental health problems.[4]

In other words, God created us for relationship. But the reason most of us do not have the relationship we've always wanted is because we've been unwilling to let go of our self-centered attitudes and grasp the concept of oneness with another person. This is especially true in the marriage relationship.

ANOTHER LOOK AT THE ALAMEDA STUDY

Remember the Alameda study, which proved how social isolation was a strong contributing factor to serious disease and illness? That study proved something else as well, something that underscores the importance of healthy relationships, especially for people whose entry point into the cycle is where weak relationships lead to poor health. The Alameda study found a profound connection between the lack of social ties and premature death from coronary heart disease, stroke, cancer, respiratory diseases, gastrointestinal diseases, and other causes.

But perhaps most amazing was that the lack of close relationships was more significant in predicting early death than were many of the things we normally associate with death, such as age, physical health, health practices, smoking, drinking alcohol, eating, and level of physical activity.[5]

In other words, whether or not you eat healthy foods, the way you relate to others may actually be the most significant factor in whether you'll suffer from long-term or life-threatening illness. Of course, if your relationships are weak, you'll also be more likely to seek love and comfort from cheap substitutes like unhealthy food choices.

In fact, researchers followed the people in the Alameda study for a total of seventeen years and found that even over a period of nearly two decades, the results remained the same. Those with the strongest social ties had dramatically lower rates of disease and premature death than those who felt isolated and alone.

This study seems to provide answers about my brother Frank. He had triple bypass surgery at age fifty-one. But he lived a completely different life from my dad and Ronnie. In other words, though Frank's food choices were not always the best, his relationships were strong enough to make up for the fact. For instance, Frank is involved in small groups. He also has a relationship with his wife in which he openly gives and receives love on a regular basis. It's the same with his kids, grandchildren, and friends. And third, he is totally involved in ministry.

As a result, Frank never needed to rely on food to fill the emotional gaps in his life. So, while he did not always eat well, he was not addicted to food by any means. Today Frank is seventy-three years old and is still going strong.

Could it be that the healing in his life was because he satisfied that God-given need to give and receive love with meaningful relationships?

A MARRIAGE OF OPPOSITES

If a loving relationship is more important for our health than the food we eat, let me give you the best information I've learned about how to have the most loving marriage, family, or friendship.

Despite my role as a marriage advisor counselor, my wife and I sometimes get stuck in our relationship. We are very different from each other. In fact, we're opposites in almost every area. I am spontaneous, with a personality marked by attention deficit hyperactivity disorder (ADHD). I am very relaxed and not usually stressed out by change. I love to be flexible. I'm not detailed and organized. Even writing a book like this, I had to get a lot of outside help in order for this book to come together because to sit down and organize it would have been almost impossible for me.

Norma is exactly the opposite. She is organized and very detailed. She enjoys working on things ahead of time and is energized by making long-range plans. She enjoys organizing our summer vacations. For twenty years Norma has truly thrived on running our ministry's front office with great care and organization.

So, here we are, living together as opposites.

Has it caused problems over the years? Sure it has. I have disagreed with her on almost everything. Likewise, she has disagreed with me on almost everything. The reason we're still very much in love today and enjoying the benefits of a lifelong marriage is because we've learned how to give and take, to consider the other person more important than ourselves, to blend. This is something I'll expand on in the coming pages.

But let me say this: If we hadn't figured out a way to blend, to live effectively with our different personalities, we might have been headed down the treacherous path to poor physical health and a greater susceptibility toward unhealthy food addictions.

SHOES ON THE CARPET

Take a closer look at Norma and me, and see if you find something of yourself in this. I remember one night several years ago when I was watching a favorite team play football on television. At one point I flipped off my shoes. As they sailed through the air, Norma looked up from what she was doing and watched them land on the carpet in front of my favorite chair.

With slightly exaggerated movements, Norma got up, grabbed the shoes, and took them into my office.

Now, I knew that my wife loves rules and that she wants our home to be clean virtually all the time. But I was thinking, *Come on. This is our home. There are only the two of us, and no one else is watching. It's ten o'clock at night, so why are you doing this?*

The reason was clear to her. She hates clutter.

That attitude amazes me. I could live in a pigpen. I could honestly live where there was so much clutter that you couldn't see the carpet, and I would be fine!

In the early years of our marriage it would irritate me that Norma was so picky. I would be bugged by her attitude, and she would accuse me of being irresponsible because I left my things lying around.

She would see my clothes on the floor or my stuff on a table, and she would think, *Gary, what if a fire started in our house or you had a heart attack or something? I would have to call the paramedics, and they would walk into this house and see your stuff lying around. I would be embarrassed if they saw this clutter!*

In the early years I can remember this happening night after night, and I would just shake my head. I couldn't believe I was living with a person who was so concerned about where things were laid. Even worse, there was nothing I could do about it. Nothing was accomplished by lecturing Norma or asking her to go to counseling. This is who she is. This is her unique personality.

But I'm happy to report that because of some of the techniques I'm about to share with you, we learned how to have the relationship we had always wanted. These days? Well, these days when I kick off my shoes at night, I usually take them into the office myself. But if Norma gets to them first, I tell her, "Thank you for providing such a great atmosphere in this home."

In this way, we are celebrating the fact that we have each other and a healthy relationship. This, then, will aid in our physical health and make us more likely to feel fulfilled, less likely to find comfort and love in false sources such as unhealthy foods.

Read on, and you'll see what happens when people are missing this key element of relationship as God designed it.

WHEN THERE'S NO ONE TO LOVE

Tanya was a woman who desperately needed the information in these studies.

At age forty-seven, the year after her two sons left home for college, her husband announced that he had been involved for two years in an affair. He left shortly after his devastating announcement. Tanya's parents had both died when she was in her thirties, so her husband's sudden departure left her utterly desolate and alone.

Tanya moved into an apartment and longed for the days when her parents might have helped her survive or when her boys were young. Night after night she stared at a photograph by her bed, crying until sleep consumed her.

The photograph, taken when her sons were in grade school, shows each of the boys hugging Tanya's neck with one hand and grasping a stuffed animal with the other. When she looked at the picture long enough, she could almost feel their arms around her again, remembering what it was to have their kisses and hugs throughout the day.

However, left alone without the benefits of relationship or physical touch, Tanya's immune system weakened. When she developed an autoimmune disorder, she was unable to recover. Two years later she died from brain cancer.

The research I cite in this chapter supports the idea that people in unhappy marriages or left alone in isolation get sicker much more frequently than married people in healthy relationships.[6] Tanya was certainly a tragic and extreme example of this truth at work.

When you think about the connection between food and love, healthy loving and healthy living, it's no surprise how damaging it is to be part of an unhealthy relationship—or without any relationship at all—but please do not give up!

If you are divorced or single or isolated or busy, if you're a workaholic and don't have time for people, you might read studies like the ones detailed in this chapter and feel hopeless. The truth is, if you see yourself in Tanya, you have hope in the most important place of all.

Why? Because the principles of giving and receiving love do not begin with our human relationships. They begin with our connection to God. A great relationship with God is more important than anything! Let's look at the conclusions from another study on how our relationships affect our physical health.

CANCER-SURVIVOR STUDY

According to one study, women who became part of a two-hour weekly support group after receiving treatment for cancer lived twice as long as those who didn't.[7] Every woman in the study who did not have a support group was dead after five years. The only women still alive were those who had participated in a weekly small-group support system. There's more information about the power of small groups in the material to come, but let me say clearly that when people are in a small group—whether the focus of that group is marriage, parenting, or some other issue—they feel loved, supported, cared for, and valuable. In small groups, people listen to each other and value what is said. That's the whole point of being in a support group.

PAINFUL WORDS FROM MY PAST

Looking back, I believe the destructive connection between food and love started for me in the way I related to other people. When people close to me would gain weight, I would feel discouraged, frustrated, and even cool toward them.

I would sometimes avoid them because I felt they lacked self-control. Sadly, I can remember saying some very mean things to those people.

From his teenage years, my son Greg recalls hearing me ridicule certain people about their weight. Today, as a psychologist, he understands more clearly the damage that was done by my disrespectful attitude toward those people. "Dad," he told me recently, "you never, ever should have talked to people about their weight like that." Greg is right.

I would tell close friends and family members that they didn't really care about themselves or their relationship with me as long as they carried extra weight. Like the rabbits in the experiment, I would isolate those people as a way of communicating my distaste for their weight problem. I tried ridiculing and lecturing these people. I tried anything I could think of.

Did I understand them? Did I seek to understand their needs?

No.

I thought my words and actions would help them eat less. It grieves me that what I thought was helping was actually hurting those people and me at the same time. I didn't realize that by criticizing them and isolating myself from them, by demeaning and belittling them, I was increasing their need to find comfort in food. In the process I was pushing them into the negative cycle involving food and love. The things I did were the worst possible things I could have done to encourage them to lose weight.

What makes me feel worse about the situation was that my attitudes and actions continued to greatly increase the harmful cycle a few of those people wound up in. I would say mean things that hurt them, but when they medicated their pain through the use of food, I would criticize that as well. No wonder I limped through several key relationships throughout those years.

I am now very convicted about my behavior. My attitudes and actions were without a doubt a huge "black eye." It was the area where I was truly blind, and now that I can see, I feel as if I'm back in the relationship game like never before.

I pray that what I've learned, the connection between food and love I've stumbled on, will help millions of people the way it has helped me.

The reality is, I truly demanded perfection—magazine-cover perfection—from most people I was close to. But I don't think I understood the full impact of the damage I did to my relationships until I started researching for this book. I also did not realize that my hurtful comments and isolation were affecting *my* health. Why? Because I was responsible for saying the words that caused separation between me and those I loved. I was hurting myself! I had fallen prey to a trap that went against what God designed when he told us to love each other the same way that he loves us.

Unconditionally.

I wish I would have known those things back then!

A LAST LOOK AT LOVE AND HEALTH

Without a doubt, God made us to love and be loved. Two separate studies show that even people whose love was primarily focused on a pet had improved health as a result.[8]

This says it all: "In summary, love promotes survival. Both nurturing and being nurtured are life affirming. Anything that takes you outside of yourself promotes healing in profound ways that can be measured independent of other known factors such as diet and exercise."[9]

Of course, God simply calls it the greatest commandment: "'You must love the Lord your God with all your heart, all your soul, and all your mind.' This is the first and greatest commandment. A second is equally important: 'Love your neighbor as yourself'."[10]

That section of the New Testament goes on to say that everything else depends on those two principles: Love God, and love others as you love yourself. It is not surprising that our heavenly Father, the Creator and Great Physician, would know what research has finally proven.

We were created to love.

And that being true, let's look at how two different people can develop a deeply loving relationship, even through disagreement and conflict.

CHAPTER TEN

Effects of Conflict and Isolation in Marriage

F or years I've counseled people who suffer from damaged relationships, and I've talked with thousands of people at seminars I've taught across the country. I have seen clearly that the relationship that seems to have the greatest impact on our health and lives is marriage.

This is true both negatively and positively. The husband-wife relationship has a profound ability to bring us health and happiness or to leave us sick and distraught.

God intends the two people joined in marriage to become truly one—one in body, heart, and soul. When that oneness is threatened by conflict or isolation, husbands and wives suffer relationally, emotionally, physically, and spiritually.

This chapter will look at ways to nurture marital oneness and to safeguard it even in the midst of conflict and isolation. I believe that a stronger marriage will lead to better health. And better overall health almost always leads to a fulfilled life, free of the need for food addictions.

Over the years I have found a powerful picture to illustrate the way two people join together in marriage to become one as God intended. That picture is the unity-candle ceremony performed at many weddings.

THE UNITY CANDLE

Did you use the unity-candle ceremony as part of your wedding? If so, did you understand what you were doing? Norma and I used it, but we didn't understand some of the richness of the symbolism of the ceremony at the time.

I believe the unity candle pictures one of the secrets to a better marriage and to stronger health as well. The greatest secret of all is oneness, the ability to let go of our status as individuals and join together with our spouse for all of life. When that oneness is lacking, husbands and wives struggle in their relationship—and in their health.

If you haven't seen the unity-candle ceremony performed in a wedding, here's how it works. Three candles are placed at the front of the church. At a time early in the ceremony, someone lights the outside candles, leaving the one in the middle unlit. The two lit candles represent the bride and groom before the wedding; they are two individuals. They walk into the church separately; they are still single.

The moment the bride and groom say their vows before God, they're not single anymore. They're married people. They are united.

The two have become one.

After the vows have been said, the husband and wife approach the three candles. They take the individual candles, and using those two separate flames, they light the center candle. The symbolism is beautiful and obvious. No longer will their lights burn for themselves alone. No longer will they live as two single people. Instead, they will enjoy one brighter light, a light that represents the oneness of marriage. The two single flames have become one.

The husband and wife have become one. They are a team, a group, a community unto themselves.

I believe the beginning of understanding in marriage comes from remembering this: When two such people leave the church, they're not separate anymore. If they continue to operate as separate people, their marriage will be doomed. The secret is learning how to blend the two in a way that will honor both partners and bring a heightened sense of unity. Hence the unity candle.

And for many couples, their unity grows in the weeks and months following the wedding. The flame of their oneness burns brightly.

But then the inevitable conflicts arise. Husbands and wives become aware of their differences, and they often don't know how to handle those differences. In their attempt to resolve their stresses, they often begin to argue and feel separate again. The flame of the unity candle, the oneness, is threatened.

I want to suggest an amazing secret: I believe that oneness in marriage is maintained not *in the absence of arguments and conflict* but *in the way couples learn how to argue.* Scott Stanley, respected marriage expert, indicates his research reveals that what keeps couples happily married for a lifetime is not how much they love each other or how much they are committed. What keeps them happily married is how they handle arguments and how they are a team throughout their marriage. [1] And the way to argue correctly is to gear solutions toward your *position as a couple,* not your position as individuals.

Read that last paragraph again. It may sound very strange at first. Most of us think that oneness is the absence of conflict. But what couple has never had conflict? Maybe only a comatose one. Seriously, though, unity is achieved when you face your conflict and move toward solutions that reflect your oneness as a couple.

Remember, it's important to learn how to argue in a marriage if your relationship with your spouse is to be strong and fulfilling. When two people toss all that they are on the table and attempt to make harmony of it, disagreements are bound to happen. And that is okay. Disagreements can be wonderfully constructive. Here's the catch: In the midst of a disagreement, the two people must examine their differing personality traits and opinions and find a way to negotiate a solution that benefits the couple, the new team.

How to Fight Right

Research I've done over the past two decades has taught me that married couples can disagree correctly if they do so *in light of their oneness.* These are key points to remember:

1. **LOVE, LOVE, LOVE.** The first step is love, unconditional love that will not be threatened by a disagreement. With this never-say-die, divorce-is-not-an-option type of love, you will be free to disagree in peace and look together for the right answer.

2. **REVEAL YOUR POSITIONS.** The next step is to explain your point of view to one another. As you do, remember that the sum is greater than the parts. In other words, your identity as a couple is more important than your individual desires, needs, thoughts, and opinions.

3. **COMMUNICATE FREELY.** Conversation and discussion about your differences are good. Explain completely your feelings about an issue and your needs. Then allow your spouse the same privilege.

4. **REMAIN MATTER-OF-FACT.** Keep emotions out of the discussion. Disagreeing is an act, not an attack. Don't feel personally damaged because your spouse disagrees with you. This means you need to keep your voice tones warm and loving, your eye contact non-accusing. Remember that the foundation you stand on is one of God-given love.

5. **ANALYZE THE DIFFERENT POSITIONS YOU EACH BRING, AND DISCUSS THEM AS A COUPLE.** At this stage, it's important to work as long as it takes until both of you understand the other's position. In my marriage, this is the step when Norma needs to understand my flexible nature, and I need to understand her detail-oriented nature. It's a meeting of the minds and a time when compassion ought to be expressed between the partners.

6. **DECIDE ON THE BEST DECISION FOR YOU AS A COUPLE.** This will require laying aside your personal individuality and taking on the goal of doing what's best to maintain oneness. It's important to reach an agreement at this stage of the discussion. If it's slow in coming, take time to pray together as a couple. My experience is that the solution will seem that much clearer. Remember, this type of healthy conversation and working through disagreements will help not only your marriage but your health as well.

7. **AGREE NOT TO BE ANGRY OR EMOTIONAL.** If you work toward a solution, but it's not really the one that you want, don't allow yourself to fret or stew about it. Remember that the goal is to find a solution that works for you *as a couple,* not one that best addresses *only your* wants or needs.

8. **DON'T LOOK BACK.** Don't keep score. And don't feel as if either of you "lost" or "won." Rather remind yourselves that you will both win every time as long as disagreements are worked out in light of oneness.

Remember: This is the only way to have the relationship you've always wanted, the one that will bring about healthy love and that will help the connection between food and love be a positive one.

HOW BRIGHT IS YOUR CANDLE BURNING?

Think about your marriage—the flame of your unity candle—and place yourself on a continuum from 0 to 100.

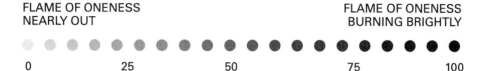

FLAME OF ONENESS
NEARLY OUT

FLAME OF ONENESS
BURNING BRIGHTLY

0   25   50   75   100

Although you will have times when you waver on the continuum, obviously the goal is to be as close as possible to 100 and a bright flame of oneness. I like to describe love like this: Listen, Offer yourself, Value and honor, Embrace. We'll discuss this acrostic in depth in the next chapter. For now just understand that a 100 position on the continuum means you and your spouse are listening to each other, offering yourselves to each other, valuing and honoring each other, and embracing each other with regular frequency.

You are at a 75 position on the continuum if you know the ways of love described above but circumstances have prevented your flame of oneness from burning as brightly as it could. Sometimes you don't really hear your spouse, don't truly think of him or her before yourself. Your marriage is generally happy, but you see room to increase your oneness.

You are at a 50 position on the continuum if you are not troubled by your marriage relationship, but you are not fulfilled either. Your marriage is just there. Believe me, this is the area that traps most people. Couples are easily fooled by the complacency that accompanies this place on the continuum. For you, I ask that you take stock of your marriage and make plans to change things immediately. Neither your relationship nor your spouse has a high priority in your life, and it's time to take action.

You are at a 25 position on the continuum if your marriage is in trouble. This point represents a marriage that is more troubled than not, more difficult than beneficial. Most people who score 25 or lower on the continuum have at least thought about blowing out the candle altogether through divorce. Perhaps you find yourself here on the continuum but have no idea how to struggle your way even to the 50 position, let alone the higher places beyond. If this is true, part 6 of this book may offer you hope and tools for lasting change. Remember, many times when serious change is needed—whether in how you eat or how you love—you will be able to do so only in God's strength.

If you've placed your marriage near the 0 position on the continuum, please know this: God is ruler over our smoldering wicks—it says so in the Bible. Listen and let the hope transfuse you: "A bruised reed he will not break, and a smoldering wick he will not snuff out."[2]

That said, your situation is still in crisis mode. Obviously, this may be the case for many reasons, some of which may be completely out of your control. Still, make a commitment to do whatever it takes to move back to oneness. That may mean professional counseling or daily prayer or understanding the simple relational steps outlined ahead. Whatever you do, do it in the strength of God, remembering that he sees your smoldering wick and stands by, waiting to help fan it into a brilliant flame of love and oneness.

FIVE DESTRUCTIVE WINDS
THAT BLOW OUT THE UNITY CANDLE

Because marital conflict actually weakens our immune systems, damaging both our relationships and our health, it's important that we take a closer look at what those conflicts are and how we can avoid their destructive power, which sometimes leads to divorce.

Do you realize we now know the five main reasons couples divorce? I call these the "five destructive winds," and I developed them largely based on research by Howard Markman, Scott Stanley, and Susan Blumberg in their book, *Fighting for Your Marriage*.[3] In that book the authors define four risk factors for divorce. I've taken those and expanded on them to create the five destructive winds that can blow out the flame of a couple's unity candle and lead not only to divorce but also to poor health.

There is the *north wind,* which escalates and can leave a crippling storm in its path; the *south wind,* which is warmer and seems soothing but leaves behind emptiness and a barren landscape; the *west wind,* which routinely brings in storms and is capable of becoming a tornado; the *east wind,* which will rarely cause immediate damage but which is irritating and constantly blows in dirt; and the *nor'easter,* which takes us by surprise and leaves devastation in its wake.

Remember, the flame of the unity candle dances brightly. But it is also easily dimmed. And when a couple isn't careful, it can be blown out. Notice something very powerful. These destructive winds blow the hardest when one of the marriage partners relights his or her single candle. People who try to remain more single than married find that their unity will become dim.[4]

In the next few pages I'll tell you about five couples who allowed these destructive winds to blow out or seriously dampen the flame of their unity candles. They are sad stories, situations that led to the weakening of these couples' marriages and their individual health.

Take a harder look at these winds, and make a commitment to avoid them at all costs.

North Wind: Escalating Arguments

The north wind builds and builds. It escalates into a fierce storm and can leave a crippling storm in its path. John and Shelly got hit by the north wind.

CAUSE: Escalating in an Argument

John comes home from work tired and weary from a day of fixing car engines. He trudges into the house and sees his wife, Shelly, in the kitchen. Without taking off his shoes or washing his hands, he comes to her and attempts to kiss her hello.

She squirms away. "Honey, you're a mess. Clean up and then kiss me."

An icy wind blows across John's heart, and he stiffens in response. "You're about as affectionate as an icicle, you know that? Would it kill you to kiss me when I come home?"

The wind touches Shelly, and she drops the spoon in the spaghetti sauce in disgust. "Listen, I work on this house all day. The last thing I need is your grimy fingerprints all over the place." She scowls hard at him. "And maybe I would be a little more affectionate if you didn't stink like a garage."

The north wind blows harder. "Fine. Great. I put in ten hours of hard labor, and this is all the thanks I get!"

"Okay, now don't get me started on thanks." The dinner is forgotten as Shelly juts out a hip and raises her voice. "You're the most ungrateful person I know! I slave around the house all day and get no thanks at all. At least you get a paycheck."

"Until you spend it on a bunch of junk!" John shouts at her.

Shelly stares at him for a minute and then allows the greatest northern gale of all: "Oh, forget it! Why did you bother to come home in the first place?" And with that she storms out of the room.

Can you hear the snuffing sound? That's their unity candle nearly going out.

Remember before the argument, Shelly was cooking dinner for John, and John wanted nothing more than a kiss. Instead, neither John nor Shelly will have the appetite to eat dinner that night, and both will go to sleep angry at the other and feeling sick. It will be three days before the ice melts enough so that they talk to each other again.

Weeks, months, and years of this behavior will do more than blow out the unity candle. It will make them sick, seriously damaging their immune systems and leaving them hungry to fill the holes in their lives with wrong habits and addictions.

Let's say Shelly decides to turn to secret eating binges as a way of comforting herself from the pain of her relationship. Years of this go by, and I don't have to tell you what the outcome will be. You already know. The woman's health will continue to deteriorate both from the damaging relationship and the resulting wrong food choices.

This is a sad picture of the predictable effects of an escalating argument, the damage possible when the north wind blows out a couple's flame—their oneness.

Escalation in an argument happens when two married people revert to defending their individual needs and agenda. When they don't consider their needs as a couple or the unity they need to protect, their flame is in danger of being extinguished.

CALM THE WIND: Avoid Escalation

Arguments escalate when a person considers only his or her personal needs and opinions and not those of the other person. Each one realizes that the other spouse has a differing point of view but believes that point of view is stupid and unnecessary.

An argument will escalate in our home if I tell Norma that her perfectionism is wrong and that my flexibility is right. Likewise, the north wind blows if I tell her to loosen up, saying things like, "You're just being ridiculous."

Escalation occurs when spouses realize that their position is being challenged. Instead of thinking of what's best for them as a couple, they get stuck on what's best for them as individuals. They become afraid that they might miss out on something they personally want or that their desires and expectations might not be met.

As spouses' anger at not getting their way increases, a chain reaction of physical consequences begins to take place. Their heart rates go up, their blood pressures elevate, and their health declines. In little time, they will see destructive results in both their marriage and their overall physical condition.

Why? Because in this scenario the escalating north wind does lots of damage. If it continues, a couple could be heading down the treacherous path toward divorce, an act that would blow out the unity candle forever.

That's the simple but powerful truth.

This type of escalation in arguing is basic to our self-centered human nature. However, real harmony in marriage comes from remembering that when we marry, we are not single anymore. By understanding that marriage must include the ability to lay our own desires on the table, trusting that our spouse will handle who we are in a way that is caring and honoring. It is agreeing to extend this same type of care and honor to a spouse regarding his or her desires as well.

In summary, remember these key points in order to avoid escalation during an argument:

- Leave your single-minded pride at the altar. It is impossible to find solutions that favor oneness when pride is in the way.
- Learn how to communicate better.
- If you find yourself or your spouse escalating an argument, draw back and give each other time and space. When emotions have cooled, try again by establishing the goal in love: oneness.

South Wind: Avoidance and Withdrawal

The south wind is warmer and seems soothing, but it can leave behind emptiness and a barren landscape. Joe and Lana got hit by the south wind.

CAUSE: Avoiding an Argument or Withdrawing

One evening as Lana is sorting through the bills and balancing the checkbook, she notices a problem. According to the checkbook, Joe didn't stop and put gas in the car. She looks up and sees him across the family room, watching college basketball on television. Lana calls to him, "Honey, did you stop for gas as I asked?"

Joe is deeply engrossed in the game and hears the question only after Lana has asked it twice. "Uh . . ." He lets his voice trail off. It's a playoff game late in the fourth quarter, and he's far more interested in the score than her question. "Yeah, I think I forgot."

Lana stares at him and sighs. Was it fair that she works on the bills while he watches a game? "You know, Joe, it really bugs me when . . ."

It's a commercial break, so Joe gives her his full attention. "What? What bugs you?"

The soothing south wind begins to blow. *Why fight with him,* Lana figures. She can always fill the tank tomorrow. "Never mind."

Joe looks at her strangely. "I hate it when you tell me never mind. If you have something to say, say it."

Suddenly everything about Joe's attitude is more than Lana can stand. But the last thing she wants is a confrontation, so she collects the bills, stands up, and glares at Joe. "Forget it. You wouldn't understand anyway."

By the time she gets upstairs, her blood is boiling, and she can easily think of a dozen things she would like to tell Joe, none of them pleasant. Meanwhile, he's downstairs hating the way she constantly huffs off by herself.

Barren places are being created by the warm south wind, and not just in Joe and Lana's love life. Avoiding an argument or withdrawing will eventually cause them both high stress and potentially high blood pressure, which could likely lead to heart disease.[5]

All Lana wanted to do was avoid fighting with her husband. But in the process, the seductive south wind blew the flame of their unity candle down to almost nothing.

This is the way the south wind works. You might think avoiding arguments is a way of saving your relationship or making it run more smoothly. Instead, you will be creating a lifeless marriage that can easily result in a house with two strangers living together. Very often this leads to divorce.

If you close off your spouse, that means you're not open. It means you're reacting like a single person again, saying, "I don't want to talk about this. It's too dangerous to talk to you. It upsets me too much, so I refuse to do this." That, in turns, sends an even worse message that says, "The person I am on the inside is private to me, and I'm not going to share it with you, so we're stuck. You can't become one with me because I won't let you."

Besides the obvious lack of communication, this behavior and mind-set causes deep anger in both spouses. Anger—especially unresolved anger—is destructive to your marriage, your emotions, your relationship with God, and very clearly it is destructive to your health. Scientific studies have shown that of all the leading causes of heart disease and strokes, the single leading cause is not cigarette smoke or a high fat diet. It's stress.[6]

CALM THE WIND: Communicate

Norma and I know how important it is to keep very short anger lists in our hearts. Therefore, we decide to talk and open up in an honoring way even when we may not feel like it. We try to take charge of our emotions and not let them control us.

Sometimes the word *stress* is used as a socially acceptable word for *anger*. When we look at anger closely, we find that it is caused by one of three triggers: fear, frustration, or hurt feelings.[7]

Lana's anger was rooted in her frustration about Joe's forgetfulness and then his unwillingness to talk with her about the problem. She also was afraid of what might happen if she pressed the issue with Joe. So she shut down.

Think of what the situation might have looked like if she and Joe would have pursued open communication about her frustration. Lana could have been willing to explain her frustration to Joe when he tried to talk with her during a commercial. Joe could have acknowledged that he had not followed through on getting gas and could have promised to hear Lana's frustration—maybe not at that moment because the game was nearly over, but he could have said, "Lana, I'm so sorry I forgot. I sense that you are frustrated. Can we talk about it in a few minutes after the game is over?"

Open communication begins by making a commitment never to bury issues. You cannot have a brightly burning flame of oneness if you are hiding emotions, feelings, and circumstances from the other person. At the same time, if you are letting outside distractions deter you from truly listening to your spouse, it may be time to check your priorities.

No television program is worth making your spouse bury his or her feelings. Especially when unresolved anger is such a destructive wind in marriage.

West Wind: False or Unrealistic Beliefs

The west wind brings in storms and is capable of becoming a tornado. Denny and Kate got hit by a west wind.

CAUSE: Holding False Beliefs or Exaggerated Negative Beliefs about Your Spouse

Denny trudges across the living-room floor with a bag of garbage in each hand. Across the room, Kate sits in a corner chair, chatting with her mother on a long-distance telephone call. Her feet are propped up, and she is taking part in a happy, animated conversation.

"Could you at least open the door?" Denny asks Kate. He hates the hours Kate spends on the phone. He waits while Kate crosses the room and does as he asked.

When he finishes the task, he returns and stares at his wife. *She's so lazy,* he thinks to himself. *Fat and lazy, for that matter. Every weekend she sits around while I do all the work.*

The longer he stands there watching her, the more disgusted he becomes. *She's too attached to her mother. She doesn't care about my needs at all. Look at her, lounging when she could be helping me. She doesn't even care about me at all. Back when we first got married she was fun and pretty and didn't talk on the phone so much and . . .*

By the time Kate gets off the phone, Denny is so frustrated with her that they have a terrible evening together, maybe even a yelling match or two. The west wind has taken its toll, worked its way into Denny's mind, and caused him to view everything about his wife through storm-clouded eyes. As a result, negativity sets in, causing tension and ultimately disease and illness.[8]

It's very likely that this will force Denny and Kate toward bad health habits as they seek to find comfort from the swirl of negativity.

Worst of all, the resulting storm will threaten to blow out the flame of their unity candle.

CALM THE WIND: Check Your Vision

If you see more negative things in your spouse than positives, you're not looking clearly and your relationship is starting to go downhill. In fact, marriage expert John Gottman of the University of Washington in Seattle says that you need a ratio of five positives to one negative in order to have a healthy, long-lasting marriage.

If this is a problem for you, here's your assignment: Get alone somewhere and write a list of every positive thing you can identify about your spouse. Here are some examples of traits that are often overlooked. He or she is perhaps faithful, honest, hardworking, consistent, funny, serious, loyal, dependable, friendly, helpful, a good cook, a good helper.

The list goes on. Look for the positives even if it takes awhile to come up with a list. If this is your struggle, you're probably out of practice, so give yourself time. The positive traits are there if you look hard enough. And remember, you'll most likely be boosting your immune system and resisting major diseases and sickness at the same time.[9] That's exciting, and it's the only way to avoid the stormy winds from the west!

East Wind: Belittling or Invalidating

The east wind will rarely cause immediate damage, but it is irritating and constantly blows in dirt. Beth and Ben got hit by the east wind.

CAUSE: Belittling or Invalidating Your Spouse

Beth is getting dressed for bed when she hears her husband, Ben, helping one their sons in the next room. The boy has been sick for the past two days, so Beth makes her way to the room. "What's happening?" Beth demands. Ben is rocking their son, but the child is coughing quite hard.

Ben puts a finger to his lips and looks at Beth. "It's okay, I have it under control. He's almost back to sleep."

Crossing the room, Beth takes the child from her husband and rolls her eyes at the same time. "He needs cough syrup; anyone can see that."

Ben isn't sure how to react as Beth scoops their son into her arms. "I would have given it to him if his cough got worse."

Beth stops in the doorway and cocks her head in a way that makes Ben feel like a dim-witted child. "If you know so much about kids, how come you forgot to put an ice pack in Jimmy's lunch today? You made him a meat sandwich, remember?" She pauses but not long enough for Ben to answer. "Meat sandwiches need an ice pack, or the kids will get sick."

Insecurity sets in, and it's the direct result of a wind from the east. Nothing strong, nothing that will cause Ben and Beth to yell and spew mean things at each other. But this incessant, nagging wind will circle around a mountain of issues and blow in dirt from all sides. It's the type of wind that sets people's teeth on edge without ever being obvious. Ben stands, scratches his forehead, and makes a last-ditch attempt. "I'll help."

Beth stifles a chuckle. "No, that's okay. You would just be in the way. Go to bed, and I'll be there in a few minutes."

When Ben turns in for the night, he isn't sure what just happened. He and Beth didn't really have a fight, but his stomach is churning all the same. When he had been alone with his son, his thoughts had been on the wonders of parenthood and the hope of sharing intimacy with his wife later that evening. Now, though, he has lost interest completely.

Without realizing it, Beth is allowing the east wind to have its way in their marriage. Day by day the resulting grit will build until finally it's too late to do anything about it, and suddenly this couple will wonder what happened to the flame of their unity candle. Of course, by then, the lack of physical love and mutual respect will have taken its toll on their health and immune systems, likely leaving them with holes in their hearts that they may very well seek to fill with wrong food choices. It's a common occurrence today, one that applied in my life and marriage, and just might apply to yours, too.

The truth of the matter is that your spouse is a very valuable person to God and others. When you belittle him or her, you are doing so to one of God's creations, to the person you loved enough to marry. Your criticisms, your faultfinding only diminish your spouse and are like the sand and grit that blows in with the east wind, endangering the strength of the flame in your unity candle.

CALM THE WIND: Speak Uplifting Words

Sometimes it's not enough to think about the positive qualities of our spouses; we must also say them aloud. Instead of letting the east wind tempt you to use your tongue to belittle or invalidate your spouse, discipline yourself to speak praise about him or her.

Use the same ratio we discussed about positive thoughts. For every disparaging word you speak about your spouse, say five uplifting and praiseworthy things. Let's look at Beth's situation. Even if she felt as if she could do a better job of caring for their son, she could have said to her husband, "Ben, you are such a tender father. You have been a real comfort to Jimmy. Thanks for giving me some relief. Even though you've nearly gotten him to sleep, I think he needs a little more cough syrup before he nods off. Shall I take him?"

Beth's words would have protected Ben's self-esteem, helped Jimmy think of his father as a valuable person, and even helped her see Ben's contribution to their family. Words that build up a spouse also build up a marriage as well as a spouse's health. These benefits are so good they cannot be compared with anything else. Several marriage experts report that rehearsing your spouse's positive assets is the best action you can take to build a strong, healthy marriage.

When you speak words of life, you are intentionally sheltering the flame of your unity candle from the dirt of the easterly wind.

Nor'easter: Withholding Information or Dropping a Bomb

The nor'easter—the rare northeastern wind that blows off the ocean and pounds the East Coast with storms—takes us by surprise and leaves devastation in its wake. Suzanne and Tom got hit by a nor'easter.

CAUSE: Withholding Information, Lying, or Dropping a Bomb

Suzanne was sitting at the breakfast table when Tom walked up to her, tossed the morning paper on the table, and said, "I haven't loved you in two years."

Never, not once in their marriage, had Suzanne seen that comment coming. She and Tom had two small children and seemed to be living the American dream.

Until that morning.

Almost overnight Tom moved out and took an apartment across town. Left with no way of supporting herself and the kids, Suzanne had to find a job and move the children into a small rental unit. The whole time Suzanne felt as if she were caught in a hurricane. How could Tom have waited two years to tell her? Didn't he love her enough to share his feelings with her back when they still could have worked on their relationship? Suzanne began using alcohol to numb her pain, and twice she tried to kill herself.

In less than a month she was suffering from the physical symptoms of depression.

This is exactly the type of thing that can happen when a couple experiences the devastating effects of a nor'easter. Not only is the flame of the unity candle snuffed out immediately with such a pronouncement, but the spouse taken by surprise is literally destroyed—emotionally and physically—in the process.[10]

The nor'easter is what takes place when one of the marriage partners has an affair or emotionally checks out of a marriage for months and years at a time. It is the bombshell announcement that often leads to an immediate separation or divorce.

Sometimes the storm doesn't always start with a bombshell. It may come after a history of keeping crucial information from a spouse or when the marriage becomes littered with lies. A married woman begins having business lunches with a single man she finds stimulating and attractive. At first she merely omits the details of her lunch when she and her husband talk at the end of the day.

But as her time with her single colleague becomes more important to her, she will almost always lie to allow herself the ability to continue having her way. Eventually, she will feel as if her husband doesn't know her, and the sad thing is she'll be right.

When that happens, the bombshell announcement is not far away.

CALM THE WIND: Avoid Letting Lesser Winds Build

In a sense, avoiding this wind is as basic as avoiding the other four winds combined. Do not allow your arguments to escalate, do not give into the temptation to avoid discussions when issues come up, do not think negatively about your spouse, and do not belittle him or her.

That may sound simple, but if you are caught in the midst of a nor'easter, you must hold on to one of the calming forces above and dig as deeply into that area as possible. In addition, if you find yourself intentionally withholding information or even lying to your spouse, it's time to come clean. Make a commitment to tell your spouse everything that's even remotely questionable. This will help keep your actions illuminated by the light of the flame of oneness. In addition, decide now never to lie to your spouse. He or she is your other half. Truth will keep you bonded together.

Don't forget: The goal is to keep the unity candle burning brightly, and keep the focus on being a couple.

MAKING YOUR UNITY VISIBLE

I would like to suggest something practical for all married people. Whether or not you had a unity candle at your wedding, I encourage you to have a unity-candle display in your home.

It doesn't have to be a fancy candelabra. It can be merely three candles grouped together, perhaps the center candle taller than the two outside ones. Choose a separate color candle to represent each of you individually, then make the candle in the middle a color that represents a blend of the two of you. For example, choose a yellow candle for the wife and a blue candle for the husband. The candle representing you as a couple could be green.

This visual display will serve as a daily reminder that the two of you have become one. It will be a symbol of your bond and oneness.

I also encourage you to light the middle candle periodically to remind yourselves that you are a couple. While doing this, pray together and commit yourselves once more to being a couple.

As you continue in a deeper understanding of the unity candle, you will find yourselves making more of an effort at maintaining your oneness.

A WORD ABOUT SMALL GROUPS

An invaluable resource that will help you preserve your oneness is involvement in a small group. Research shows that small groups offer an opportunity to share feelings and concerns, provide accountability, develop social ties, and enhance relational skills. You will experience these benefits, whether you are part of group that is a Bible study, a couples' group, or a weight-loss group.[11]

Small groups seem to help us better understand how we actually allow Christ to live his life through us by watching and hearing how others interact. That being the case, we're better prepared to take those truths, wrap them in God's loving kindness and mercy, and share them with our spouse.

Norma and I are part of a small Bible-based support group made up of four couples. That group offers us a sense of strength and well-being that research is only now beginning to understand. In all my years of ministering to couples, I don't know of anything better for renewing and enriching your marriage than being in a small support group. Married people will always do better together if they have a small-group outlet.

One of the most exciting things we've seen happen in small groups is having couples write their own Marriage Constitution, which outlines clearly and practically how couples promise to love each other throughout life.

We at the Smalley Relationship Center have helped thousands of couples write out personal constitutions made up of four to ten articles. Here are a few examples of the articles people have written:

1. We promise to keep oneness our primary goal through God's strength and love and mercy—not our own.
2. We promise to listen to each other actively, with eye contact and uninterrupted attention.
3. We promise to rely on God to help us truly understand each other.

In the personal-constitution-type small group, couples meet weekly to exchange their articles and discuss the practicality of each one. They help each other clarify and apply the articles. Once each couple feels comfortable living out their constitution, they may elect to start a new small group and help other couples do the same. If you want more practical help and information on this, log on to our Web site—Smalleyonline.com—and click on to the marriage constitution section.

A FEW POINTS TO REMEMBER

Here are a few final points about creating a healthy marriage relationship:

- After the wedding ceremony, you are not single anymore.
- Understand that you were created for relationship.
- From the first day of marriage, you will be happier and healthier if you make decisions and solve disagreements based on what's best for you as a couple.
- Do not allow arguments to escalate.
- Discuss your differences when disagreements arise.
- Think positive thoughts about your spouse.
- Commit to being open and honest about all aspects of your life and your marriage. Watch for a buildup of smaller problems and deal with them as they arise.
- Say uplifting things to and about your spouse.
- Set up a unity-candle display in your house to symbolize your oneness.
- Join a small group that will help you grow.
- Remember the goal: Keep the unity candle burning.

Now that we've taken a look at how conflict and isolation can weaken our health, let's explore ways that we can strengthen our relationships in ways that will also lead to greater physical health. As I mentioned earlier, when we love and are loved deeply and fully, we have the best chance at physical and emotional health. The next chapter will outline four skills that will help you love more fully and leave you less likely to reach for a chocolate sundae in order to feel loved and satisfied.

CHAPTER ELEVEN

L-O-V-E: The Cure for Conflict and Isolation

W hat you are about to read regarding improving your relationships should be read this way. Say to yourself, *This is the way I want our relationship to be someday, and I can hardly wait to see God give me both the desire and the ability to live it out.*

All four of the following love skills by themselves can eliminate the five destructive winds that blow out the unity candle and destroy marriages, winds I believe most of you easily identified with. Just think of it, you can use each one of these skills and be confident that you won't be blowing out or dimming your flame of love on your unity candle. In the process, you will go a long way toward eliminating the need to love yourself with processed food products and other cheap substitutes.

Of course for many of you, these skills—just like the ability to eat healthy foods—will be impossible to implement in your own strength. But then, that's what part 6 of this book is about: learning how to act in God's power through the seven steps to lasting change.

Okay, let's get down to business.

As you try to understand these four love skills, remember them in light of the unity candle. The goal, you'll recall, is to experience a deeper relationship with your spouse by allowing your individuality to blend in a way that makes a brighter flame, a fire of oneness. The key here is this: Always be receiving love and mercy from God; always be extending love and mercy to your spouse.

For the purpose of better understanding what it means to love, I've come up with an acrostic that defines the areas that most often need work in struggling relationships.

L I S T E N

O F F E R   Y O U R S E L F

V A L U E   A N D   H O N O R

E M B R A C E

Let's take a moment and learn how to apply these skills to our relationships—especially our marriages.

1. LISTEN

You cannot under any circumstances have an intimate, satisfying, emotionally and physically healthy relationship unless you communicate. Remember the research from earlier chapters? Isolated, noncommunicating people are sick more often and are more likely to die of serious illness or disease.

One of the keys to effective communication is listening. The Epistle of James in the New Testament encourages us, "My dear brothers and sisters, be quick to listen, slow to speak, and slow to get angry."[1]

Listening involves two very important steps: *hearing* and *understanding.*

When two people try to communicate, they bring their individual needs, concerns, and expectations. Real communication will occur when those two people are committed to hearing and understanding the other person's needs, concerns, and expectations. Did you catch what I just said? The primary goal is to hear and understand *the other person;* the goal is not, first of all, to be heard or understood. However, if both people are committed to real communication, both of them will be heard and understood in the process.

Think about your communication with your spouse. You come to each other with your ideas, your hopes, your frustrations, your fears, and your needs. What happens then? How can you hear one another and attempt to understand, as clearly as you can, your spouse's point of view?

First, let your spouse speak. Your initial goal is to hear what he or she is saying. Make direct eye contact. Do whatever you can to encourage your spouse to express his or her thoughts or feelings. Don't correct your spouse; don't respond to what you hear. Just let your spouse know that you hear what he or she is saying.

Then transition into understanding. Spend as much time as you need to make sure you understand your spouse's point of view. Ask questions that will help you determine if you have understood your spouse's words. "I want to make sure that I understand you correctly. Is this what you mean?" Then give your spouse a summary of what you heard.

Often after I have summarized what I think Norma has said to me, I will ask her, "Am I clear on this, or have I missed the point?"

She often will say, "No, you've missed the point. Let me explain it differently. Maybe I can use a word picture to help you understand what I'm saying." Then she will try another method to explain her thought or feeling in different words.

I'm 100 percent responsible to understand, and she is 100 percent responsible to explain it in a way that I can understand. It is important not to give up until you find a way to understand each other. Ask as many questions as necessary to help clarify your spouse's intent. Do whatever it takes to understand.

Did you hear me? Are you *listening?*

Don't skim over that last part, because it's absolutely crucial. Keep probing and listening to your spouse until you really understand what he or she is saying.

Here's an example: Several weeks ago, Norma and I spent three or four hours talking about some changes happening in our business. First, I listened to her needs and concerns. As she talked, I wrote down what I understood her to be saying. To make sure I was clear about her meaning, I repeated to her what I heard her saying.

I took all that I had written down and really tried to feel her feelings and understand her point of view. We used word pictures to communicate as well.

Next, I told Norma my list of needs and expectations, and I wrote them down. Then we analyzed each other's lists.

This is nonthreatening because we aren't saying we agree with each other completely at this point. The objective is simply to understand the other person's feelings. We think things through and value each other's opinions, and in that way we are able to truly listen, truly hear each other.

After that we discussed possible solutions in light of our oneness, our unity. I feel safe to share what I think and feel, and she feels safe to share what she thinks and feels. As I understand her needs and she understands mine, we both will be thinking of ways to resolve our differences. We look for solutions that would make us both feel valued and honored, solutions that would benefit us as a couple first and foremost, regardless of what our individual needs might be.

That, my friends, is a picture of true listening and oneness.

Often your spouse simply wants to know that you are listening and that you understand. Sometimes that in itself can solve the whole thing. That's the amazing thing about open communication. It is so powerful!

It is so powerful because we are vulnerable, connected, and committed. We're in love, and this type of communication increases our love for one another. In fact, the truth is, where God's love and mercy grows, pride isn't found. And pride is the ticket to feeling single in a marriage—the most dangerous risk to the relationship and therefore to the physical health of the couple because of the likelihood to seek love through the false method of poor food choices.

Listening with humility and love is the picture of intimacy and a beautiful illustration of a deep, healthy relationship.

2. OFFER YOURSELF

Research has shown that if you offer yourself to your spouse, you are more likely to enjoy a healthy, long-lasting, loving bond. As we've already seen, this, in turn, will lead to a healthy body and greatly reduce the need to choose unhealthy foods as a means of false love and fulfillment.

What if you're married to someone who doesn't want to offer himself or herself? The principle still holds. Although it's difficult, try to be less concerned with what the other person in the relationship is doing for you and more concerned with what you are doing for him or her.

Again, in many relationships this may be possible only through God's strength. We will learn more about living in that strength in part 6.

Twenty Minutes to Marital Bliss and Better Health

According to marriage expert John Gottman, there is great reward for people who spend at least twenty minutes a day offering themselves to someone they love. Research shows that such a selfless investment in time and energy separates couples who are happily married from couples who end up divorced.[2]

The first step to making these twenty minutes effective is to know your spouse's needs. Set aside a few hours one night for you and your spouse to write down a list of your needs. If you are married to someone who doesn't want to try this, you may have to work harder to know his or her needs.

Even so, it shouldn't be too difficult to find a way to serve and nurture your spouse's needs for twenty minutes each day.

For some people that may mean carrying on a conversation when you're too tired to talk or walking around the block when you're too tired to walk. It might mean actively listening more or giving the kids a bath before bedtime. Whatever it is, identify your spouse's needs and then work on meeting them wherever possible—offering yourself to the one you love—for at least twenty minutes a day.

Yes, you will have times when this love skill is difficult to carry out. Remember though, with God's love and mercy you can tell yourself this: *Reading this information is wonderful, and I am going to trust God that through his love and timing, this is how my marriage will actually look one day.*

Then simply continue to seek him daily, thank him daily, and honor him daily.

Try this exercise: Set aside an evening when you and your spouse can take separate pieces of paper and write down endings to this sentence: "I feel loved when you . . ." Do not limit yourselves. If you can fill up two pieces of paper, do so. This will provide you both with a gold mine of information on how to understand each other's relational needs.

3. VALUE AND HONOR

Giving value and honor to someone is giving distinction to that person, giving worth to him or her. The New Testament reminds us to "be devoted to one another in brotherly love [genuine affection]. Honor one another above yourselves."[3] Similarly, Philippians 2:3 directs us to think of others as better than ourselves. It's similar to the principle Jesus taught when he asked us to love our neighbors as we love ourselves.

Recognize that your spouse's opinions are very valuable, even more valuable than your own. For instance, with Norma and me, I had to understand that the beauty of our oneness was found in blending her unique personality with my unique personality. Our marriage has grown tremendously since I've started valuing and honoring her, cherishing her personality traits that are different from mine.

I truly believe this is a difficult thing to do in our own strength. Why? Because our human nature is selfish, much more concerned for our own well-being than that of our spouse. Sometimes the last thing we want to do is honor or value our spouse. Without God's help, we might be angry and frustrated and ready to walk out the door—possibly even out of the marriage.

If you've never been able to find lasting success in your relationship, the seven steps to lasting change in part 6 may make it possible to find victory by God's power, not yours. In the process you'll have a better understanding of oneness and finally be able to separate yourself from . . . well, from yourself.

Journal of Honor

One of the most effective ways I have found to value and honor people is to keep a lifetime journal. I encourage you to do the same. Buy a quality keepsake-type book, and call it your journal of honor.

Start by writing about God. Tell him why you value and highly esteem him and love him more than anyone or anything else. When Scripture says "Bless the Lord, O my soul; and all that is within me, bless His holy name,"[4] the word *bless* means bowing to God, bending your knees in front of God. It means that in your mind there's nothing on earth higher than God. As you write in your journal, list the reasons why you esteem God above everything else on earth.

Then move on to the reasons you value and honor your spouse. Start making a list of all the reasons why your spouse is important to you, why his or her uniqueness is valuable. My wife's perfectionism—a quality that caused friction in the early days of our marriage—is now high on the list of assets that I consider priceless.

In my journal of honor, I have more than five pages full of all the reasons why my wife is so valuable to me. I keep the list close at hand, and I often tell her why I value her. It is one way I can honor her.

According to Mark Goldstein, medical instructor at MIT, writing out the reasons you value your spouse is the best way to relight the unity candle if you are a couple struggling with marital problems. Counselors will often give such a couple only one assignment: "Go home and start listing positive things about your spouse, and then share these things together." Seventy percent of those couples improve and continue to improve over time.

Remember the food-love connection? When our relationships improve, our overall health improves as well. Improved health means we will be less likely to seek out processed foods to provide ourselves with artificial love and fulfillment.

Three Steps to Valuing and Honoring Your Spouse

To summarize the process described above, let me list the three steps to showing value and honor to your spouse.

1. Make the decision to recognize that he or she is a highly valuable person.
2. Make the list of things you value about your spouse. When starting your list, write down every good thing you can think of. Then add to the list each week. For a romantic evening, read some of your list to your spouse. If he or she is making a list about you, your spouse may be willing to share that list with you.
3. Verbalize on a regular basis why he or she is so valuable to you. This might mean praising those traits when they come to mind, putting sticky notes in your spouse's purse or wallet, surprising him or her with a list of their positive qualities, telling children and friends—both in your spouse's presence and away from his or her presence—why you value your husband or wife. Believe me, when it gets back to your spouse that you've bragged about him or her, it will be a real boost to your partner's self-esteem.

Sadly, our human tendency is to focus on the negative qualities of our spouses. What they lack. How they could look better. How they could love better. How they aren't meeting our needs.

By shifting our focus to what's good and right and excellent about our spouses, our negative thinking actually reverses, and we will begin to see our spouses differently. Watch how that strengthens your relationship and makes you more grateful for each other.

4. EMBRACE

Without a doubt, physical touch remains one of the best ways to convey love. I first discussed this in my book *The Blessing* (with John Trent), and I must say that I believe as strongly in it today as I did then. The little hand holds and brushes of the finger on your spouse's arms or face, the hugs and kisses, and skin-to-skin contact will always be a way to convey a thousand words about love.

Physical touch tells your spouse, "I love you, I need you, I like you. You're worth a lot to me, and I don't want you to go away."

Remember the rabbit study described in chapter 8? The more physical touch you can extend to each other, the healthier you will be in absolutely every area of your life.

By the way, since physical touch is crucial to any healing process, I thought I would include here a list of ways you can use touch to love your husband or wife.

Ten Ways to Add a Touch of Love to Your Marriage

There's nothing like physical touch to make us feel loved, accepted, and desired.

1. Hug when you see each other at the end of the day.

2. Work in the kitchen together, laughing and talking, and let your arms brush against each other now and then. Stick your hands in the same warm soapy water so that your fingers touch on occasion.

3. Take too much lotion for your hands, and ask to rub the leftover cream onto your spouse's hands.

4. Offer to give your spouse a hand massage, working your fingers into the tendons and muscles of your spouse's entire hand.

5. Sit together when watching television or a movie. If your spouse sits in an easy chair, try the floor between his or her legs. This way you have contact with your spouse's body throughout the show.

6. Offer to give your spouse a massage.

7. Hold hands when you're driving in the car together. Make up a private sign—such as three hand squeezes—to communicate I love you.

8. Kiss more often. Freshen your breath, soften your lips, and have at it. Remember how much fun you had kissing before you were married? Why stop now?

9. Allow yourself to be intimate in places you haven't thought of before—the clothes closet, the shower, the kitchen. Spontaneous touch is always a good thing.

10. Don't grope without warning. There's nothing more irritating to most women—especially if they're struggling with their weight—than to be bending over doing something with, say, the dishwasher when you come up and give them a pinch. This is not a good type of touch for most women.

The benefits of physical touch are so tremendous, there's simply no reason to wait. Try these on your spouse today, even if he or she isn't doing anything to improve your relationship. You'll be surprised at how fulfilling an embrace between you and your loved one will be.

The alternative, of course, is a relationship where one or both of you feel isolated or hurt. It's in these types of relationships that many people find themselves turning to cheap substitutes as a way of finding false love and fulfillment. What's our culture's favorite cheap substitute? Unhealthy foods, and lots of them.

In the connection between food and love, the next segment of the cycle is the notion that our overall physical and emotional health affects our food choices. Read the next section, and see if you or someone you love is perhaps eating the wrong foods as a way of filling holes in the heart.

PART 5

OUR EMOTIONAL AND PHYSICAL HEALTH AFFECT OUR FOOD CHOICES

CHAPTER TWELVE

Cheap Substitutes for Love

H ave you ever wondered why so many people struggle with food addictions and other similar abuses? Of course, many factors come into play, but one that needs more discussion by psychiatrists and therapists is that our poor relationships have led to poor physical and emotional health, and that, in turn, has created huge holes in our hearts. How do we fill those holes? How do we very often seek to find love and fulfillment when our relationships are not loving and fulfilling enough? Gregory Jantz, head of an eating-disorder clinic in Washington, has said that the leading cause of eating disorders is relational dysfunction.[1]

For many of us the answer is food. We navigate our way through the days of our lives barely surviving from one sugary overload to the next. Some of us become binge eaters in our attempts to find love and fulfillment. Others of us merely eat cookies and candy and processed doughy products as a means of rewarding ourselves, thereby avoiding the healthy foods we might otherwise be eating.

At this point, we've discussed our God-given need for healthy relationships, particularly the marriage relationship. But what happens when our marriages aren't what they ought to be? In this chapter you'll travel with me down a frightening road, a road that too many of us have journeyed and perhaps are traveling even now.

It is the road of cheap substitutes.

When we don't have healthy relationships, we develop holes in our hearts. As I said earlier, those holes must first be filled by a vibrant relationship with God. Nothing else will satisfy us on a deep level.

The void grows larger when our relationships with the loved ones in our lives are shallow or unfulfilling. This lack creates a void that can be filled only by making the relationship healthy.

But some of us spend years, decades, even a lifetime filling the void with cheap substitutes, some of which are downright dangerous.

- Food addictions
- Eating disorders
- Illicit or wrong relationships
- Drug or alcohol addictions
- Other addictions

These are commonly used to meet our emotional needs at times when weak relationships leave a vacancy in our hearts. In a sense they reflect ways we medicate ourselves from the pain created by those holes. We will take a deeper look at each of these in the pages to come.

WHEN FOOD IS LOVE

At an early age Stephanie learned that food was love. As far back as she can remember, her family used food as a means of reward, entertainment, comfort, and love. It wasn't that her parents were trying to do something awful to Stephanie and her siblings. Rather they passed along what they knew, and it wound up looking like this.

When Stephanie and her siblings went on day trips or vacations with their family, the outings always revolved around "stopping for a treat." Sometimes it was a milk shake near the waterside or an ice-cream cone at the park. Other times it was fast food with an extra order of onion rings if the kids had been particularly good.

If Stephanie and her sisters and brother came home with good report cards, their dad would take them to see a movie. The family wouldn't see much of the show, however, as they gorged themselves for two hours with bonbons, popcorn, sodas, and licorice. "You kids deserve it," their father would say with a smile. "You've been so good this semester."

This reward system carried over to the grocery shopping as well. Stephanie and her sister would help their mother make the rounds up and down the aisles, pushing the cart and collecting things off the shelves as their mother directed. At the end of the trip—if they were good—they would be rewarded with the opportunity to select any candy bar they wanted and eat it on the ride home.

Stephanie can't remember a time when they weren't "good" enough to get a candy bar. As they grew into their teen years, the candy bars grew until Stephanie and her siblings were allowed huge chocolate bars, the types most people break into squares and eat slowly over a long period.

Food wasn't only a reward for being good. It was also a way of showing comfort. When Stephanie was sick or injured in any way, her mother would slip an arm around her shoulder and guide her into the kitchen. "Let's bake cookies, honey. That'll make you feel better." The same means of comfort carried over when the pain was caused by a bruised heart rather than a skinned knee or a high fever.

Stephanie was nearly sixty pounds overweight by the time she entered junior high and was clearly caught up in the negative cycle that can come as a result of the connection between food and love. The foods she ate had made her heavy and harmed her self-image. In the process she had become isolated by her peers, and as a way of numbing the pain of loneliness, her mother routinely directed her back to food.

Small wonder, then, that by the time I saw Stephanie, she was still caught in the negative cycle. Her marriage was suffering, and the only way she knew to reassure herself of her "goodness" and to comfort herself from her lonely marriage was to keep eating the same unhealthy foods that had harmed her in the first place.

I talked to one couple where both the husband and wife needed to lose close to a hundred pounds. The woman described their situation perfectly: "We've always bought into the idea that food is love," she told me. "When we wanted to show love to each other, we bought each other candy bars or treated ourselves by going out to dinner."

Today they have recognized the cycle that exists between unhealthy eating and unhealthy loving. As a result, they've placed their energies into learning how to L-O-V-E better (Listen, Offer yourself, Value and honor, and Embrace). Finding strength from God, they helped each other learn how to eat healthy foods in moderate amounts. Today they are both at normal weights and have a marriage their friends and family members envy and admire.

The trouble is, when people turn to cheap substitutes instead of investing themselves in loving relationships with God and others, addictions can crop up. When that happens, it will be only by God's strength that lasting change will be possible.

Let's take a look at some of the ways cheap substitutes can literally consume us, taking over every aspect of our lives.

FOOD ADDICTIONS

In today's world, the easiest and most common substitute for real love is food. If you doubt this, read some of the survey results people have given me at various seminars (see appendix B). My personal journey to health has involved my reading more than four dozen books about food and love. In the process I've learned one thing very clearly: *God has designed us so that we eat to live.*

But far more than half the people in this country have that backward. Unable to work out their relational differences, unaware of the destructive winds that can blow out the flame of their unity candles, too many people push through life at breakneck speeds, using food for everything but sound nutrition. In other words, they are living to eat, in many cases hoping to find the love and fulfillment they are missing in their relationships with God and others.

When I asked people at my seminars why they ate certain foods, their responses were not surprising. In fact, their responses line up with a general understanding that resonates in our society today.

Most people use food:

- to comfort themselves,
- to give themselves a reward,
- because they're frustrated,
- because they're bored,
- as a pastime, or because it's fun.

The list goes on, of course, but these reasons come up time and time again. Take a look at the list. Each item involves a person trying to satisfy himself or herself, trying to fill a hole meant to be filled by God.

The trouble is, God didn't create that hole to be filled with food. He created the hole to be filled first of all by a loving relationship with him and second by loving relationships with others.

When these same people at my conferences were asked what types of food they use to fulfill themselves this way, their answers were again predictable:

SWEET FOODS. Sweets topped the list. This included ice cream, cookies, baked goods, candy, and chocolate. These are also the foods most likely to lead into a food addiction and/or bingeing.

WHITE BREADS. These include doughy foods such as pizza, garlic bread, dinner rolls, and pastries.

FRIED OR FAST FOODS. Many people spoke of stopping at a fast-food restaurant, ordering a large meal, and eating when they weren't even a little hungry. Why? To treat themselves in some way.

SALTY FOODS. This was another popular one. Potato chips, corn chips, pretzels, popcorn, and salted nuts were among the favorites.

The problem here is obvious, and the results are predictably devastating. The reason so many of us have fallen victim to making substitutions for healthy love is that we pacify our God-given relational needs with unhealthy foods and health habits. To make matters worse, this behavior is almost always cyclical and can worsen with each passing year.

ONCE AGAIN, THE TERRIBLE CYCLE

We've talked about the terrible cycle so many people are caught in, but let's go over it once more from the perspective of people who feel trapped in loveless relationships.

- The more our relationships—particularly our marriages—leave us feeling empty, the more we seek to fill the void with wrong foods or poor health habits.
- The more we fill the void with wrong foods or health habits, the more unhealthy we become.
- The more unhealthy we become, the more our emotional health is harmed.
- The more our emotional health is harmed, the more likely we are to struggle in our relationships.
- The more we struggle in our relationships, the more we turn to poor foods or other cheap substitutes for fulfillment.

On and on the cycle goes until something devastating happens: a divorce, an affair, a heart attack, a life-threatening disease, or something else.

Again, the reason I wrote this book is because it is possible to find a breakthrough if you're caught up in the negative cycle. With God's help, all things are possible. Keep that in mind as you continue toward the last section of this book.

What happens when our food addictions are allowed to spin wildly out of control? For many people the next step in that destructive pattern is an eating disorder.

EATING DISORDERS

An eating disorder is often a food addiction or food abuse problem that has escalated to the next level. Typically a myriad of emotional causes trigger an eating disorder, but ultimately it is our subconscious attempt to fill the void we feel from an unhealthy relationship.

The following most common eating disorders can be dangerous at best and deadly in some cases.

BULIMIA. Bulimia is a condition in which a person self-induces vomiting as a way of ridding his or her body of food. Very often people with bulimia experience periods of self-starvation followed by periods of massive gorging. I know of a young woman whose father was a football coach. There were four daughters in the family, and Anna was the youngest. She tried everything she knew to get her father's approval: competitive sports, shared outdoor hobbies, and adoration. When nothing seemed to work, she turned to bulimia. By the time this young woman checked into an inpatient program for help, she was unable to drink a glass of water without triggering her vomiting reflex.

EXCESSIVE OVEREATING OR GORGING. Picture a Thanksgiving when you forgot to remind yourself to stop eating. You ate the appetizers of crackers and cheese, olives and pickles, chips and dips. Then you ate a meal with ten or more food items. If you topped it off with a sampling of two or three different pies, you probably know what it is to gorge yourself. For most people, this might happen only one or two times a year. But for people looking to fill an unmet relational need with food, overeating or bingeing can take place every week—sometimes every day. Ryan suffered from this disorder. He had trigger foods, moods, and situations that would set off a binge regardless of where he was or who he was with. On his forty-second birthday Ryan learned that he had adult onset diabetes, a disease that can lead to blindness, limb amputation, heart disease, and early death. His doctor told him that his disease was the result of excessive overeating, which had worn out his body's pancreas and ability to produce insulin.

ANOREXIA. This condition is brought on by long periods of self-starvation along with an unrealistic assessment of body image. Lynette, a college student, had suffered the breakup of an engagement to a man she deeply loved. He told her he thought she needed to lose five pounds. As a way of pacifying or medicating her pain and loneliness, she began skipping breakfast. Soon she was skipping both breakfast and dinner. When she collapsed in class one day and had to be rushed to the hospital, her daily food intake consisted of three glasses of water and an apple.

If your relationships with God and others are unhealthy and if you have dabbled in food addictions or abuses as a way of fulfilling your unmet needs, you may struggle with an eating disorder. Please know that professional counseling—preferably Christian counseling—along with consistent prayer is the only answer for these types of disorders.

Another helpful resource is *Hope, Health, and Healing for Eating Disorders* by Gregory Jantz. As I mentioned earlier, he says that all eating disorders are caused by unresolved past hurts in relationships and that this primarily starts in our family of origin.[2] One of the themes this book deals with is how parental habits—especially a mother's habits—tend to carry over to the children.

Jantz says the mother of a person with an eating disorder is often very controlling and may have her own history of dieting or food abuse. Tending toward perfectionism, this mother—or on occasion a father—will likely have rigid ways of thinking and relating to others. She may put an exaggerated importance on weight, her own and her children's. "If you're the mother of a child and you behave in such a way as I describe, the chances of your child developing an eating disorder are greatly increased."[3]

Fathers who are emotionally distant and isolated contribute to their children's eating disorders, Jantz says. These men have very high expectations of their children.

On the other extreme, a parent who is too close, overbearing, enmeshed in every detail of a child's life, and perhaps involved in an inappropriate physical or emotional relationship with the child is also a contributor to eating disorders. Sexual abuse, for instance, is a major factor in a girl's developing an eating disorder as an adult.

Finally, the use of guilt or shame to control a child's behavior can contribute to eating disorders. I have found that the same is also true in a marriage. If the woman is living with a very controlling, critical, domineering, self-seeking husband, then that hurt can separate her, isolate her, and cause her to develop a great friendship with a secret friend called food.

Let's just take a look at a few of the other ways we attempt to meet our relational needs with substitutes.

ILLICIT OR WRONG RELATIONSHIPS

This substitute applies especially to a weak or failing marital relationship. When you allow the winds of destruction to blow out the flame of your unity candle, you will limp through life with a gaping hole in your heart. As I've said, it's a hole created by God, and the only healthy solution is to allow him to fill it. But people often seek to medicate the pain of a failing marriage by developing secret friendships or outright illicit sexual relationships. This is very dangerous territory!

Adultery—or sex outside the marriage—is clearly forbidden in the Bible for our own good. Nothing will destroy a marriage faster than this type of substitute for a healthy relationship. At the same time, it is also one of the most seductive ways of fulfilling unmet needs.

Charles fell prey to this very trap. In the first five years of marriage Charles allowed each of the destructive winds to blow through the heart of his home. The oneness he should have shared with his wife had long been extinct when he met Laura, a coworker at his office.

Because Charles had not taken care of his or his wife's marital needs, he went through his days with huge needs that cried out for fulfillment. Laura was funny, friendly, and attentive, full of compliments and frequent pats on the back. One night while both Charles and Laura were working late, their conversation drifted from work to more personal matters. Before going home that night, Charles spent nearly an hour kissing and holding Laura. A week later he was involved in an affair that eventually cost him his marriage and caused a breakdown in his immune system. Research says that if you are isolated and in great disharmony with others, you increase your chances of developing a major disease like cancer by more than 60 percent.[4]

There is no doubt that initially, Charles believed his relationship with Laura was the answer to his problems. But now that he's had a chance to step back and look at the destruction his choices have caused to his family and his health, he knows he fell for a lie.

He bought into the quick fix and lost everything as a result. If Charles had understood his need for a healthy marriage and if he had been taught the principles of oneness we discussed in the previous chapter, he would have done everything he could to apply these truths to his relationship with his wife.

If you see yourself in this story, keep reading.

Sadly, Charles's story isn't too different from that of countless people who have chosen to fill the hole in their hearts with other addictions.

OTHER ADDICTIONS

One of the easiest ways to tune out when relationships begin falling apart is to misuse drugs and alcohol. Many people—even people with deep religious beliefs—find themselves using these substances to numb the pain of loneliness, boredom, anxiety, and other painful emotions.

This often leads to alcoholism or drug addictions, which can destroy marriages and entire families in a very short time. Obviously, this type of addiction also has a direct relationship on a person's health, and it begins a cycle that grows constantly worse.

If you or someone you love has tried to fill emotional, relational voids with drugs or alcohol, seek professional help. Although the material in the last section of this book may help you, serious illness, injury, and death can result when people addicted to drugs and alcohol do not get help quickly.

Many people turn to many other addictions to fill their emotional needs. Excessive shopping, talking on the phone, gambling, buying on credit, and even healthy habits like exercise can make us unbalanced. While these addictions may appear to be less serious than food addictions or alcohol and drug addictions, they are definitely harmful and can leave us susceptible for a serious nor'easter—the type of wind that will destroy us with little warning.

If you have seen yourself in this chapter and if you have looked to cheap substitutes, don't be discouraged. No matter what you might have used to medicate yourself from the pain of an unhealthy marriage or other unhealthy relationships, it's a pattern you don't have to be a part of anymore.

The answers lie just ahead.

They can change your life.

CHAPTER THIRTEEN

Ten Ways to Extend Grace When Weight Is an Issue for You or Your Spouse

Sherri walks into the room and models a new pair of jeans for her husband, Frank. "I'm down a size, can you tell?" Her face is bursting with pride, her self-image better than it's been in months.

Frank cocks his head and studies her. "You're still losing, right? I mean you're not stopping there are you?"

The comment twists its way into the holes in Sherri's heart, and she retreats to their bedroom. There she remembers some of the things her husband has said to her in the past.

The time when she told him about a friend who had lost weight: "She'll gain it back just like every other woman I know."

The time when she was cleaning out the closet: "You used to look so good in that straight skirt. I never thought you would let yourself get heavy again."

The afternoon when she joined him for an ice-cream cone at the pier: "So are you starting another diet Monday? You usually eat like this when you're about to start a diet."

The time when he didn't want to make love for several days in a row: "Your weight doesn't mean I don't love you as much, honey. I'm just not as attracted to you."

That night Sherri cries herself to sleep remembering the hurtful things Frank has said over the years.

And she's not alone. Millions of people can relate to comments very much like these.

In talking with thousands of people at my seminars and having them fill out surveys, I discovered something that won't surprise you, at least not this far into the book: One of the most common issues of conflict in marriage involves the relationship between food and physical health. This includes issues of overeating, poor eating habits, excess weight, and fitness concerns.

Since 70 percent of the people in this country are overweight and since our media continue to throw images of half-starving women at us and tell us they're the norm, I am absolutely certain most of you will relate to some aspect of the stories in this chapter. The theme is the same in each: How we love affects what we eat, and what we eat affects how we love.

Just to underscore the point, I would like to share some more survey results from my recent seminars.

QUESTION: How have your spouse's eating habits affected your relationship?

- I tried to change her eating habits and made negative comments about her eating.
- It causes arguments.
- My husband has gained weight in the last few years and seems to be eating uncontrollably. I am concerned and don't know what to say to him.
- My husband has damaged our relationship because he overeats. He gets sick a lot and promises that he is going on a diet. His weight is affecting our sex life (no sex—impotence). I tell him he is killing himself and won't be there for our three kids ten years from now. He needs to do something quickly and set this as a high priority.
- I am angry with my husband at times because he looks good in anything he wears. He doesn't understand what I go through as I stand in front of the closet and cry because I am heavier than I want to be.
- Weight gain makes my wife feel self-conscious, and it restricts what we do and where we can go.

The next survey question shows the degree of addiction many people face when it comes to unhealthy eating. For although we clearly admit the problems that poor health and eating habits can cause in our marriages, we also clearly understand the benefits change would bring.

QUESTION: What positive impact would eating healthy foods have on your relationship?

- It would help reduce my weight and my spouse's occasional embarrassment.

- We would be healthier and more energetic and be able to focus on the positive aspects of our marriage.
- We would have more energy, more strength, and less sickness.
- I would feel better mentally and physically because of what I eat. I would treat others differently.
- I would have more energy to play with my children, do housework, and have sex.
- When I eat healthy foods, I have energy. I look and feel better. Being healthy, I believe, is a reflection of our relationship with Christ.
- We would have more unity of spirit, mutual support.

These are people who attended my seminar, not experts on the connection between food and love. But read their answers again. They understand the truths I've been talking about in this book. What they're probably lacking is the ability to let God make it happen in their lives. We will discuss the key to tapping into God's power in part 6.

MARRIAGE PROBLEMS THAT ARISE

I have counseled many couples whose marriages have been damaged by weight issues. It's typical that when these couples sit in my office, the immediate assumption is that if only the overweight person would lose a certain number of pounds, everything would be fine in the marriage.

That is simply not true. I agree that if weight is an issue, a reduction in that weight will help. But it is not the only solution.

If one spouse is overweight, both people have a problem. Both spouses need to work toward a solution. And I believe that the responsibility of the spouse who is not overweight is just as significant as that of the overweight spouse. The overweight person struggles with food; the other spouse struggles with his or her reaction to the overweight spouse. Both struggles are important.

Far too often I see angry, frustrated husbands and wives who are impatient with overweight spouses. In their impatience these husbands and wives are often unkind, rude, and disrespectful toward their spouses, ridiculing them, belittling them, devaluing them. That behavior is just as serious as the overeating that results in the excess weight. And as we have seen in earlier chapters, these behaviors often drive the overeating spouses even further into the cycle of using food to find comfort and self-esteem.

For the rest of the chapter I would like to look at the needs and struggles of the overweight spouse as well as the needs and struggles of the husband or wife living with the overweight person. My prayer is that after reading the rest of this chapter, you will have a better understanding of your spouse and will gain empathy for the struggles he or she faces.

As you read, set aside your frustrations with your spouse and allow God to show you how you can love him or her more deeply. Ask the almighty Surgeon to carefully cut away the hard places in your heart and give you the grace to be a helpful force in your spouse's life.

THE OVERWEIGHT SPOUSE

Jo Ann loved people. From the time she was a little girl she craved attention and loved conversation, social gatherings, and get-togethers. The more people the better.

For as far back as she can remember, her family's fun times centered on lots of people and at least as much food. And whether it was the result of eating habits or a predisposed problem, by the time she was in junior high school, Jo Ann had a serious problem with her weight.

To the tune of "Batman," the kids in her third-period health class would sing, "Fat-girl, fat-girl, fat-girl . . ." whenever she walked into the classroom. Fifth period wasn't much better. Once when the teacher was late to class, three boys conspired at the chalkboard and wrote, "Jo Ann. Fat lady at the circus. Now showing in the back of the room."

If Jo Ann hadn't been so social, the gaping hole in her heart might not have been so painful. But she was, and she seemed to find just one way to medicate her pain: She would eat.

During lunch, while the social, more popular kids sat together at a group of six or seven tables, Jo Ann sat across the cafeteria by herself, eating the same thing every day: a cheeseburger, large fries, and fresh-baked brownie. If there was time before the bell rang, she would slip back into line and get another burger or another brownie.

Of course, food had a way of being her friend one minute and her enemy the next. Her weight ballooned up to more than two hundred pounds when she was in seventh grade, leaving Jo Ann with a wardrobe of stretch pants and maternity tops.

Most days, she would walk home from school quietly wiping tears from her cheeks.

Then, just after Christmas that year, she was struck by a thought. She didn't have to eat like that. She could change what she ate and lose weight! So she read a few dusty books in her parents' library and adopted a program that caused her to lose nearly eighty pounds before high school started.

Overnight she was the popular girl, the thin girl—the one the boys wanted to get to know and the girls wanted to befriend. That was fine and good until she gained back five pounds and one of her friends told her this: "You would be so pretty if you would just lose five pounds."

That comment sent Jo Ann into a tailspin that resulted in a three-year struggle with bulimia. It seemed that no matter what she did, the problem was the same. Jo Ann longed for social acceptance and involvement but could only have it on conditional terms.

The bottom line was this: She felt loved only when she was thin.

Sadly, these feelings carried over into her marriage. She was the perfect weight at the wedding, but a month after having their first baby, Jo Ann still had forty pounds to lose. Every day her husband, Bart, seemed to grow further from her, and although she very much wanted intimacy, he was uninterested most of the time.

One day Bart told her why. "I'm just not attracted to you. You used to be so . . . well, so thin."

It wasn't that he nagged her every day about what she ate. He didn't have to. His silent rejection was more devastating than anything he might have said. Frustrated, depressed, feeling alone and rejected, Jo Ann turned to the same old seductive friend—her food addiction.

After their second child was born, Bart became more vocal about Jo Ann's struggle with weight and food. At a wedding reception of a friend of theirs, he said, "Are you sure you need that piece of cake?" At dinner with another couple, he nagged, "Honey, maybe you should skip the bread, huh?" And at an ice-cream parlor after their son's league championship football game, he commented, "You don't want an ice-cream cone, honey. You're cutting back, right?"

Every comment he made distanced her from him that much more. The pain was so great that she had no choice but to cut herself off emotionally from him, allowing their marriage to become one of function and convenience. She still needed the love and social interaction she had craved as a child, but because of her weight her husband was sending her the same message she had always gotten: I'll love you only if you're thin.

One day Jo Ann found a marriage book on her husband's nightstand. As she flipped through the pages, she saw an underlined section that said a husband needs a thin wife and that she must be physically attractive or the marriage doesn't have a chance.

Jo Ann wept as she read the words and wound up starving herself for two days afterward, but her addiction came back stronger than ever.

By the time she sought professional help, she was 125 pounds over-weight, her marriage was on the verge of destruction, and she had been diagnosed with hypertension and varicose veins. In addition, she suffered from an anxiety disorder and occasional bouts of depression. Her health was falling apart, and her emotional and spiritual health were falling right along with it.

The battle raged. The harder she tried to stop overeating, the more difficult it became. Eventually it became an addiction far greater than any force she had ever known. Looking back she realizes that she did not rely on God's power as much as she needed to, but at that point she had no under-standing of that power and no way to allow it to work in her life.

The night before she suffered a heart attack, she wrote this in her jour-nal: "Deep inside me is a person no one knows, an invisible person. A little girl who only wants to be loved. And no one, not my husband, not me, not even God himself knows how to let her out."

Thankfully, gratefully, Jo Ann's heart attack did not kill her. Instead, it caused her to do the very thing I did when I reached the end of my rope with overeating. She cried out to God and told him that she was clearly beyond herself. No longer could she even try to break her addictions herself.

I'm happy to report that today Jo Ann has lost most of her weight. In the process, she and Bart have gone through marriage counseling and have learned how to extend grace, mercy, and loving-kindness to each other.

A Word to the Overweight Spouse

Just so you know, I understand some of your pain. I know what it feels like to have the button on my pants snap open in the midst of a dinner party because of my expanding girth. I know what it is to eat without the ability to stop and to go to sleep at night consumed by feelings of inadequacy and guilt.

But now that I, too, have walked through the miry swamps of overeat-ing and struggling with weight, I can say this: Excess weight is an issue that we must take 100 percent responsibility for. Yes, you might be predisposed to gaining weight. You might be trapped in a bad marriage or a hurtful rela-tionship. You might be completely unable to lose weight in your own strength. A dozen reasons already discussed in this book might be the cause of your weight problem. Still, you are the one who lifted your hand to your mouth and fed yourself the food that caused you to gain weight.

Hard as it may be to take the path of trusting God and waiting for him to bring you a breakthrough in this area, it is important that you own what *is* yours. The Bible assures us that "Nothing is impossible with God."[1] You can and will find victory if you take the steps to allow God to work in you.

In terms of your marriage, explain to your spouse that you need his or her support. If your spouse is like Bart and has ridiculed or belittled you, explain that those things hurt you.

Ask your spouse to forgive you for overeating, and ask him or her to pray for you, joining you in waiting and watching for a miracle to overcome this battle. Pledge to start using more of the L-O-V-E skills in your marriage, or join a small group to increase your ability to love each other.

Then think about what your spouse is going through because of your weight problem. Empathize. Try to have mercy for your spouse, especially if he or she has been unkind to you about your weight problem. Learn to extend grace to your husband or wife.

Ten Ways to Extend Grace to an Unkind Spouse

Grace and mercy are crucial in any marriage, but they are especially needed in a marriage where one of the partners is struggling with a food addiction or excess weight. Remember, the better your relationship is, the easier it will be to fight the "battle of the bulge."

Here are ten ways to help understand your spouse, while helping him or her to better understand you:

1. Realize that your husband or wife doesn't understand your sensitivity about your weight.
2. Consider writing him or her a letter or having a deep conversation in which you talk about your food struggles and weight struggles as far back as childhood. This is not something you do lightly or in the heat of an argument. Rather it can be a way of softening your partner's heart toward issues he or she may never have understood before.
3. Believe that your spouse is not rejecting you when he or she makes an offer of help.
4. Let your spouse help. Ask him or her to pray for you or to avoid bringing certain foods into the home.

5. Be loving! When we imagine we're being rejected, it is easy to withdraw love as a consequence. This will snowball quickly.

6. List your spouse's assets, and give honor by complimenting him or her. When your focus is on extending love and mercy, it will be off you and your vicious cycle of dieting or overeating.

7. Find common interests and schedule playtime together.

8. Realize that your weight affects more than your looks. It could also leave your unkind spouse planning your funeral if your weight seriously threatens your health.

9. Agree that God wants you to experience his good health and energetic life. Believe that through his power, change in your health and eating habits is possible.

10. Begin to pray for a breakthrough.

How My Attitude Hurt Others

I mentioned earlier in this book that my attitude toward people who struggled with weight and food issues had been less than understanding. I thought I would give one of the people close to me a chance to share personal feelings about the matter. Thankfully this person has forgiven me and has even been able to thank God for the way the issue has strengthened our friendship.

Nevertheless, the real and painful feelings this person felt are worth sharing.

"Yes, Gary's attitude hurt me. He would comment on my weight or my eating, and I would get a feeling of fear inside, fear and frustration and pain that seemed to come right from my heart. The ironic thing was that his words and attitude simply increased my desire to eat more as a way of soothing my emotions. This is what anger does, and I was very angry and very hurt by his comments.

"His actions could have weakened our friendship in that I distanced myself from him during those hurtful times. At times I wondered whether I would ever feel close to him, safe and cared for unconditionally for who I was inside.

"Here he was telling other people about how to have great friendships and relationships, and I felt as if he was suffocating ours.

"Those were dark times, but God turned the light on for me so that I was able to forgive Gary. I would tell myself that he didn't know what he was doing and that God wanted my response to be that of forgiveness.

Honestly, through God's grace alone I did not walk in bitterness through that stage of our friendship. Because of that, we're still friends today. Best of all, after years of praying and waiting, God gave me the relief I had been waiting for the day Gary realized the depth of my struggles with weight, and he was able to apologize to me for his attitude."

THE OTHER SPOUSE

Bob knew that Rosa's family had a problem with weight, but he wasn't worried. The day he married Rosa she was a size five, and he figured she would stay that way forever. Not because she was under some obligation to do so, but because she was an aerobics teacher who valued physical fitness as much as he did.

Even after Rosa gave birth to their two children, she maintained her weight and stayed in shape, working out at the same health club where she once taught classes. But when Rosa turned thirty-five, something changed.

She complained about not having time to exercise. She had a new job doing medical transcriptions on her home computer and was involved with her kids' school and church activities. But Bob noticed Rosa always seemed to have time to bake cookies or cakes or brownies.

The weight began piling on at a rate of about two pounds per month. At the end of the first year, Bob was silently growing alarmed. Not only had Rosa lost her cute and curvy figure, but she seemed to complain more often of aches, pains, and other ailments.

He chose a Sunday afternoon to first address the subject. "Honey, are you getting worried about your weight?"

Rosa's face became red, and Bob wasn't sure if she was going to cry or scream at him.

"I've got my weight under control just fine, thank you." She spat the words at him, stood up, and retreated to their bedroom.

Bob sat there alone in the dining room and blinked. If he couldn't talk to her about the problem, what was he supposed to do? He began thinking up ways to talk to her without making her upset. The next weekend he tried a new approach.

"Hey, let's play tennis this afternoon." He came up beside her and poked her gently in the side where a modest roll of fat had begun to form. Subconsciously he hoped to convey the point that exercise might help her lose the fat.

Rosa jerked away as if she had been slapped. She busied herself with the dishes. "I . . . I don't feel like playing tennis. My back hurts."

Bob felt frustrated. After all, he was only trying to help her. But he was starting to get the picture. The topic of Rosa's weight gain was off-limits.

They could talk about his day at work or her day with the kids. They could talk about the ways in which he needed to help more around the house. But they must walk around her weight issue as if somehow it didn't exist.

One day he broke the unspoken rule and took her in his arms. "Honey, what can I do to help you with your weight problem?"

Immediately he felt her stiffen beneath his touch. "Are you saying you don't think I'm attractive?"

Her tone was short and angry, and Bob struggled to make sense of her reaction. "No, but I think we need to talk about it. I would like to help, but you keep pushing me away."

Rosa's eyes filled with tears, and she turned away, trudging upstairs without saying another word.

It wasn't long before Rosa's twenty pounds became forty, and forty became sixty. Because she wasn't very tall, sixty extra pounds put a considerable strain on her system. Once when she tried to jump down from a kitchen stool, her knee gave out, and she wound up on her back for a week. Over the next month the joint was never without pain, and finally doctors learned that she had torn her ACL—the anterior cruciate ligament, which keeps the kneecap in place and the joint working correctly.

In the waiting room of the hospital the day Rosa had knee surgery, Bob couldn't help but think that the entire ordeal was caused by his wife's overeating and excess weight. He sighed and let his head drop, his eyes focused on the floor. Rosa was the love of his life, and he would do anything to help her. He would help her buy healthy foods, make a work-out plan with her, encourage her to stay away from junk food. Whatever she needed.

But for reasons he couldn't even come close to comprehending, Rosa had put up a ten-foot thick barrier on the issue of her weight. Because of that, Bob felt that they were growing cold toward each other. He was so frustrated he wanted to scream, so isolated he wanted to tear into her room and tell her there could be no off-limits conversations in their marriage anymore.

Instead, he merely closed his eyes and let the feelings pass. Rosa had made her position clear. If her overeating and weight continued on like this, he knew there was a good chance the distance it would place between the two of them could ruin their marriage.

But obviously it didn't matter much to Rosa. After all, she was the one with the problem, and if she didn't want help, if she was satisfied with watching their relationship crumble, then there wasn't much he could do about it but stand by and let it happen.

Sadly, that's exactly what happened, but not in quite the way you might think. Two years after Rosa's knee surgery—a time when Bob would make an occasional suggestion to Rosa about what to eat or how to be more active—she suddenly latched onto a weight loss program and shed nearly a hundred pounds. She had tremendous energy, and every single one of her physical ailments disappeared.

Although Bob and Rosa had attended church in their younger married days, neither of them had been committed to a relationship with Christ. They also had not understood even a little of what his grace and mercy might mean in their marriage. When Rosa was looking her best, she began secretly dating the single parent of one of the kids' friends. A year later, she and Bob divorced. When they signed the final papers, Rosa leveled her gaze at Bob and said, "You loved me only when I was thin. I just couldn't live with that anymore."

Bob's jaw dropped, and he stared at her in shock. What did she mean he loved her only when she was thin? He had loved her through every added pound, through her sicknesses and ailments, and lack of interest in their physical relationship. Emotion welled in his throat, and he swallowed so he could find his voice. "I never stopped loving you. I was only trying to help."

A Word to the Other Spouse

In many ways I understand the pain you are experiencing. I have heard countless couples tell me about the roller coaster of emotions they feel as a spouse starts a diet—the hope when the diet begins, the painful disappointment when, once again, that diet fails.

Having listened to people who have walked this side of the fence, I feel compelled to warn you about the purpose of this book. This information was never intended to be used as a weapon against the overweight spouse. Please do not read this material, track down your overweight spouse, and say, "Gary Smalley says you are ruining yourself. You may die or wreck our marriage. It's time for you to change!"

Many overweight people have suffered at the hands of insensitive, unkind spouses. The last thing I believe God wants from this book is to pour gasoline on those spouses' already hot fire of contempt and disappointment over their overweight spouses. There are devastating, lasting consequences for unkind people who continue to emotionally wound their overweight spouses.

Basically, that's what I did to some of my friends and family members. I spent a great deal of energy trying to change their eating habits because they irritated me. I thought that if they wouldn't eat so much, our relationship would be better and I would be happier.

I failed to understand that the things I found irritating in overweight people were God's way of showing me where I needed growth within myself.

Trying to change my loved ones only weakened our relationship. The weaker our relationship became, the more they needed to medicate their emotional pain with an increased need to continue their "irritating habit." Psychiatrist Gerald May says that all addictions are caused by weak relationships.[2] With my lack of knowledge in this important area, I did not extend grace to my loved ones, and our relationships were not what they could have been.

Today I can only thank God that I finally started seeing the problem and taking responsibility for it.

Remember, it is crucial that you take responsibility for the hurtful things you've said or done in the past, things that you hoped would spur on your spouse to a diet that would finally work. I speak from experience when I tell you that it is next to impossible to battle weight and wrong eating on sheer willpower alone, and the resulting failures are devastating enough without barbs and jabs from an unkind spouse.

Examine your past behavior. Perhaps it's time to seek forgiveness for the ways in which you've tried to manipulate change from your overweight spouse. Pray for God's patience and grace as you try to understand what your spouse is going through in his or her struggle with weight.

Empathize. Try to have grace for your spouse, especially if he or she has tried countless times to lose weight.

Pledge to start using more of the L-O-V-E skills in your marriage. Ask God to give you kind words and to prompt you to love your spouse through tender touch.

Let's take a look at how you can extend grace to your overweight spouse.

Ten Ways to Extend Grace to an Overweight Spouse

1. Make a list of the things you like about your spouse.
2. Compliment him or her by using this list.
3. Be physically affectionate. Touch your spouse tenderly in areas that will not call attention to his or her excess weight.
4. Limit your intake of sugar and processed foods in an effort to be a good example to your spouse.
5. Determine your spouse's comfort level about the issue. Some people can talk about their weight, others can't. If your husband or wife is comfortable, talk about it.
6. Let your spouse know that you love him or her unconditionally—no matter what. Use the L-O-V-E steps to strengthen your relationship. The more loving your relationship, the more likely your spouse will desire a change.
7. Encourage your husband or wife to open up to you about personal feelings. Be sensitive about your wording.
8. Avoid poking or pinching areas of fat. This is a very loud unspoken sign of rejection.
9. As much as possible, praise your spouse's looks.
10. Look for ways to have fun and laugh together. This will take the focus off the issue of weight.

Now I realize that sticking to a list like this can typically be done only in God's strength. If you have deep concerns for your overweight spouse or are struggling with your lack of physical attraction to him or her, take this matter to the Lord. Cry out to him. As you humble yourself, he will lift you up. Pray for your spouse's breakthrough to good health. Although this may not happen in a week or month or year, at least by extending grace and mercy, you can have a beautiful relationship while you wait.

WHAT IF . . .

How did you respond to Jo Ann and Bart's story? How did you react to Rosa and Bob's story? I pray that they have helped to soften your heart.

Sadly many people do not know about God's desire to take our struggles upon himself. If they did, they would learn some truths in the process.

In addition, many people haven't learned what it truly means to L-O-V-E. In Jo Ann's case, Bart could have found reasons to honor or validate her, reasons that might have let her know that his love for her was more than superficial. As for Rosa, she had a way of turning Bob into the bad guy when the truth was she had her own issues to deal with. Her overeating was only a small problem compared with the way she refused to communicate.

What if Bart had shown Jo Ann physical love and touch despite her excess weight? What if he had tried to understand her past and the way she had never quite felt accepted by people unless she was thin?

What if Rosa had put aside her damaged pride and given Bob an answer to his question about how he could help her?

TREASURE HUNTING THROUGH THE PAIN

Through the years of our marriage, Norma and I have learned a spiritual discipline that may help you as you work through marriage problems that may have arisen because of weight problems. We have learned how to thank the Lord during any painful or hurtful periods.

Together we have learned that when we are hurt, the only real damage is done by how we respond to the pain. If we get bitter over time, that choice decreases our marital satisfaction and weakens our immune systems, opening us up to sicknesses and diseases. But if we thank the Lord for the pain and let him develop our capacity to love more, then we grow in our relationships and our health improves.

We get better, not bitter.

Note the difference in the spelling of these two words. *Bitter* is spelled with an *i*, which stands for "I think I've been hurt," basically a self-centered attitude. *Better* is spelled with an *e*, the first letter in the word *Emmanuel*, God is with us. He's right there beside us in the midst of the greatest pain. He's with us and for us. And if God is for us, who can be against us, right?

Both of us have had painful areas in our lives, and we have learned to hunt for the treasure in the pain. The good news, though, is that both of us always got more loving after these hurtful experiences. After I struggled with my weight, I allowed God to use that pain to make me more empathetic to others. I've become more empathetic. I feel another's pain even if I haven't had exactly the same experience. I know more how to help people work through their pain because I have had to do it.

There is truly an endless list of benefits to handling painful experiences by being grateful to God and looking for him in the midst of a painful time.

Ask God to show you the benefits of your marriage struggles. Quite often he uses trials to bring more love into our hearts and move us toward being more like him. The New Testament reminds us, "Dear brothers and sisters, whenever trouble comes your way, let it be an opportunity for joy."[3]

Remember, the secret to healthy love, healthy living, and a healthy relationship with the Creator is this: Always receive grace and mercy from God; always extend grace and mercy to your spouse.

I pray that the Lord will allow you to find joy as you work together toward a healthy, whole marriage relationship.

The next few chapters will move you along the path to finding the key to lasting change, both in your eating habits and in your relationships.

PART

6

STEPS
TO LASTING CHANGE

CHAPTER FOURTEEN

If Nothing Else Has Worked

T he simple truth is that most of us can't bring about change in our lives by ourselves. If we could, all we would need to do is follow a set of rules. The more rules we had, the more success we would find. In no time at all we would be eating healthy foods in healthy amounts and taking time to practice the skills involved in true L-O-V-E (Listen, Offer yourself, Value and honor, and Embrace).

But that isn't the case. If you doubt this, take a look at the ways in which rules have failed us in the past.

EXERCISE AND DIETARY RULES HAVEN'T MADE US HEALTHIER

If you struggle with your weight and have tried one diet, you've probably tried a dozen. By now many of you could probably write a diet book of your own, but the truth is that even if you wrote it, you probably couldn't follow it.

Diets involve a list of food and calorie restrictions. They teach us rules, head knowledge about what formula to follow to see the pounds melt from our bodies. Sounds simple enough. But the reality is that only 5 to 10 percent of people who diet will keep off their weight.[1]

When I heard this fact, I was startled by a truth that comes straight from Scripture. "But sin took advantage of this law [these rules] and aroused all kinds of forbidden desires within me! If there were no [rules], sin would not have that power."[2]

In other words, by our very nature we are driven to fail when in our own strength we try to live by a list of rules. The same is true when it comes to making our relationships work.

RELATIONAL RULES HAVEN'T MADE US LOVE BETTER

Each year I could write five new books about loving your spouse, and I still would have a large percentage of readers whose marriages would fail. Indeed, the divorce rate among Christians is even slightly higher than that of non-Christians. Divorce happens to couples who seem to have the perfect marriage. Divorce happens to famous couples, and it happens to couples in leadership roles in the church. I love Promise Keepers because the leaders urge men to go home and love their wives and families better. But they never fail to point out that it's not going to happen without God.

You know the stories of tragic marital failures, especially the ones that make us shake our heads: the Christian leader whose ministry involves marital counseling, the pastor who had preached a dozen sermons on faithfulness, the perfect neighbors who seemed as if they had everything together. The list is depressingly long.

How, we ask ourselves, is it possible for that man, that woman, that couple to fail? We reason that this particular leader or that certain teacher should have known all the answers. They had access to books and lists and programs and rules. But still they failed. And we wonder why.

The answer has everything to do with the essential message in Scripture. Most people are basically helpless on their own. They do not have the strength, stamina, or ability in their own power to make their relationships work.

Rules and laws fail. God's people have never been able to live by the law, and that's what we'll see here.

GOD'S RULES DIDN'T MAKE US LIVE BETTER

Before Jesus died on the cross and sent his Holy Spirit to empower people to live godly lives, God gave his people rules by which to live. He gave rules about what to eat, what to wear, whom to marry. He gave ceremonial laws, relational laws, and hygiene laws along with many, many others. But time and again throughout history, people broke the rules.

What we see in the Old Testament is a continuous cycle, not unlike the ones we get stuck in today when we are ignorant of our great dependence on God.

God would provide a law. The people would break the law. God would punish the people and/or require a sacrifice to cleanse them of their sin.

God would reestablish the law. The people would break the law. God would punish the people and/or require a sacrifice to cleanse them of their sin.

You get the picture.

The entire futility of those methods is summed up in the New Testament: "The old system in the law of Moses was only a shadow of the things to come, not the reality of the good things Christ has done for us. The sacrifices under the old system were repeated again and again, year after year, but they were never able to provide perfect cleansing for those who came to worship."[3]

This problem of law giving and lawbreaking continued until the time of Jesus Christ. In fact, it continues to this day in our rules and laws about diet, relationships, and society.

I think sometimes we're tempted to disdain the people in the Old Testament for being wanderers and grumblers, failures at keeping God's law. But when we look at how we fail the laws and rules we try to live by—even those we *want* to live by—it's very clear that we're just like the people in the Old Testament.

LAW LEADS TO DEPRIVATION

If you look back over the last few pages, you'll see that every time laws are instituted, people are expected to give up something. Relational laws ask us to give up our individuality; diet laws ask us to give up foods we enjoy; exercise laws ask us to give up our time and energy; spiritual laws ask us to give up our selfish desires.

Each of these laws makes us feel uncomfortable or deprived, as if we're missing out on something fun or good or tasty or enjoyable. The fact is, we don't like to deny ourselves. We hate being deprived. The reality is that every cell in our body will kick and fight against us when we or someone else imposes laws on us. It's a direct result of our sinful nature.

In the apostle Paul's letter to the Romans, he describes his struggle with sin. The passage is full of do's and don'ts, but we find a crucial biblical truth there. Let's take a look at that passage from a contemporary paraphrase:

The law code started out as an excellent piece of work. What happened, though, was that sin found a way to pervert the command into a temptation, making a piece of "forbidden fruit" out of it. The law code, instead of being used to guide me, was used to seduce me. Without all the paraphernalia of the law code, sin looked pretty dull and lifeless, and I went along without paying much attention to it. But once sin got its hands on the law code and decked itself out in all that finery, I was fooled, and fell for it. The very command that was supposed to guide me into life was cleverly used to trip me up, throwing me headlong. . . . But the law code itself is God's good and common sense, each command sane and holy counsel. . . . Sin simply did what sin is so famous for doing: using the good as a cover to tempt me to do what would finally destroy me. . . . I've spent a long time in sin's prison. What I don't understand about myself is that I decide one way, but then I act another, doing things I absolutely despise. So if I can't be trusted to figure out what is best for myself and then do it, it becomes obvious that God's command is necessary.

But I need something *more!* For if I know the law but still can't keep it, and if the power of sin within me keeps sabotaging my best intentions, I obviously need help! I realize that I don't have what it takes. I can will it, but I can't *do* it. I decide to do good, but I don't *really* do it; I decide not to do bad, but then I do it anyway. My decisions, such as they are, don't result in actions. Something has gone wrong deep within me and gets the better of me every time.

It happens so regularly that it's predictable. The moment I decide to do good, sin is there to trip me up. I truly delight in God's commands, but it's pretty obvious that not all of me joins in that delight. Parts of me covertly rebel, and just when I least expect it, they take charge.

I've tried everything and nothing helps. I'm at the end of my rope. Is there no one who can do anything for me? Isn't that the real question?[4]

Sounds like deprivation to me. I should know; I've spent most of my life walking a similar path. And I suspect that you have, too. But read on, because where law brings deprivation and opportunity for sin, God has something far better planned for those who will trust him.

GOD PROMISES TO HELP US
If we believe in God, in his word and his promises, we can embrace a life that includes lasting change in the areas of food and love. How? By relying on his strength. We no longer are relegated to working out our own solu-

tions to life's problems. Not the problem of poor eating habits or the problem of weak relationships.

Let's take a look at some of these promises:

- "Not by might nor by power, but by my Spirit," says the Lord Almighty.
- "I can do everything with the help of Christ who gives me the strength I need."
- "But you will receive power when the Holy Spirit comes on you."
- "I advise you to live according to your new life in the Holy Spirit. Then you won't be doing what your sinful nature craves. The old sinful nature loves to do evil, which is just opposite from what the Holy Spirit wants. And the Spirit gives us desires that are opposite from what the sinful nature desires. These two forces are constantly fighting each other, and your choices are never free from this conflict. But when you are directed by the Holy Spirit, you are no longer subject to the law."
- "When the Holy Spirit controls our lives, he will produce this kind of fruit in us: love, joy, peace, patience, kindness, goodness, faithfulness, gentleness, and *self-control*. Here there is no conflict with the law."
- "Loving God means keeping his commandments, and really, that isn't difficult. For every child of God defeats this evil world by trusting Christ to give the victory."
- "For Christ has accomplished the whole purpose of the law."[5]

IN GOD'S STRENGTH ALONE

Are you ready? It isn't a matter of redoubling your own efforts, buckling down, and forcing yourself to love your spouse more. It will never be a case of trying harder in order to see that diet work.

The answer is simple. We must give up our own efforts and embrace what the Spirit is doing in us through God's strength, not ours.

We must let go and let God.

That's right, we don't have to muster the strength to change; God will give us change from within. Change will actually feel easy when God is doing it.

I know, I know, you're thinking this all sounds wonderful, but how in the world are you supposed to tap into that supernatural strength? The answers to that question are listed in the next chapter—one of the most exciting chapters I've written in all my life.

God has made his strength available to us in all areas of our life, if only we would learn how to ask for it, wait for it, and live in it. I'm about to share with you what has worked for me: the seven keys to tapping into God's strength in making lasting changes both in the way we eat and the way we love. Don't be surprised if God's strength creates in you, your health, and your relationships the same type of breakthrough it created in mine.

WHAT EXACTLY IS GOD'S POWER, ANYWAY?

Tim wanted desperately to be a runner. As a young child Tim would watch professional track events, his eyes wide as he studied the winged feet of the graceful runners.

The fact that Tim had Down's syndrome didn't matter to him. He wanted to fly around a track and feel the wind in his face and the finish line in his arms. The same way his father had when he was a boy.

Tim's father had been a track star through high school and college, and many of his sprint records outlasted two decades of athletes who came after him.

"I'm gonna run just like that one day, Daddy," Tim loved to tell his father, "I want to be just like you."

The father would choke back tears and smile. "That's right, Son. One day you will."

There was a problem with Tim's dream, though.

When Tim ran, he tripped. Even when he would try to run merely across the living room, his feet became hopelessly entangled, and he would crash to the floor.

Once in a while at Tim's request his father would take him to the local junior high school so he could practice on an actual track, but the results were always the same. Tim would take several jerky steps and fall hard to the ground.

The fact was, no matter how hard Tim tried, he always wound up tripping.

Years passed, and the summer the boy turned eight a Special Olympics event came to town. Tim's father agonized about whether to register his son for the hundred-yard dash, but finally he knew he had no choice.

"I'm going to run like you, Dad," Tim told his father minutes before the race, his face lit up with possibility.

Tim's father hugged him close and nodded. "I'll be right here to see it, Buddy."

As the runners took their place, Tim's father moved off to the side, his eyes glued to his son.

"On your mark, get set, go!" The gun sounded, and Tim took off alongside the others.

His father's response came with neither forethought nor hesitation. He simply started running on the outside of the track, step for step staying even with his son.

Not ten yards into the event, Tim noticed his father, and a smile filled the child's face. At first his dad's presence seemed to give Tim an added sense of sureness. Then, just before the halfway mark, Tim's right foot landed squarely in front of his left, and he tumbled to the ground.

A collective gasp came from the parents and spectators in the stands. Tim's father ran to his boy, scooped him into his protective arms, and sprinted the remainder of the distance, crossing the finish line before any of the other runners.

The crowd was on its feet, clapping wildly for the father-son team and the victory they had managed together. As Tim's father held him, the boy took hold of his father's hand and thrust it high into the air, his smile radiating throughout the stadium. "Thanks, Dad!" he shouted above the sound of the applause. "Today I ran just like you!"

That, my friends, is a picture of what God wants to do for us.

He's our heavenly Father, and we're just like Tim, struggling and tripping and barely able to run ten yards through the trials of life without falling. Ah, but our Father never asked us to run on our own power. He has the strength to carry us so that we, too, can cross the finish line victorious. How?

On his strength, not our own.

The exciting thing for you and me is that Jesus agreed to do all the work when he gave up his life for us on the cross. That very act released a power that is greater than anything in our world, anything anyone has ever known or imagined.

The power of God.

I've written this section of the book to teach you how to tap into a power that is bigger and greater than your own, a power that is from God alone, a power that will allow you to do something you could never have done otherwise.

GOD'S STRENGTH LEADS TO OPPORTUNITY

If we look again at Paul's letter to the Roman Christians, we will notice that he doesn't end his discussion about the power of sin and the futility of the law by tossing his hands in the air and walking away. No. He wanted his listeners to understand that he had been there. Like them, he struggled with sin and in some ways always would. But he ends chapter 7 with this celebratory line—the line that gives us reason to hope, reason to turn the pages of this book and expect a supernatural breakthrough: "Is there no one who can do anything for me?" Then he answers his question this way: "The answer, thank God, is that Jesus Christ can and does."[6]

Pondering further about the inability of the law to change our behavior and the marvelous freedom in living in God's strength, the apostle says, "The law always ended up being used as a band-aid on sin instead of a deep healing of it. And now what the law code asked for but we couldn't deliver is accomplished as we, instead of redoubling our own efforts, simply embrace what the Spirit is doing in us. . . .

"So don't you see that we don't owe this old do-it-yourself life one red cent. There's nothing in it for us, nothing at all. The best thing to do is give it a decent burial and get on with your new life. God's Spirit beckons. There are things to do and places to go!"[7]

MY NEW APPROACH TO READING THE BIBLE

This new awareness of God's strength and power has led me to a breakthrough in how I read the Bible. I find myself excited to read it because it speaks to me in a new way. As a lifelong Christian I've always understood the necessity of reading the Bible and spending time in God's Word. Like most people, Scripture has often jumped off the page, shouting and screaming and making immediate application to my life.

However, I also have had times when reading the Bible would leave me slinking in my chair, feeling as if I had failed God. In fact, at times reading the Bible was like chewing sand. I would feel things such as, *I shouldn't have thought that thought* or *I shouldn't have said those things* or *I should have acted differently* or *I should have done more.*

The older I got, the more I found myself slinking rather than thinking. More often than not I allowed God's Word to make me feel guilty for not "performing" as I should have. I was as incapable of living a godly life as I was of flapping my arms and flying.

Then about two years ago I began understanding that no growth would ever come about in my life because of my own strength or because I had read a list of do's and don'ts. Change would come about only as God gave me the ability to change. It would happen in his strength, not my own.

Since I was struggling with overeating at the time, God's power applied there as well. I could not change my ways and lose weight, couldn't eat differently and become healthy without relying on God's power in that area of my life. I was like Tim, tripping up at every turn. But when I learned how to rely on God's power and strength to get me through, it was like having my eyes opened for the first time, and it had an immediate effect on my Bible reading time.

Now when I read the Bible, it's with eyes wide and full of excitement. The reason? I'm not getting a list of all the things God expects me to do and be on my own. Remember the old saying, "Please be patient with me. God is not finished with me yet"? That's how I feel now when I spend time in Scripture. *I'm getting a picture of how I'm going to look when God finishes working on me.*

"Wow!" I often say as I read the Bible. "That's how I'm going to look when he makes me into the Gary Smalley he wants me to be!"

After all these years of loving Christ, I finally understand that everything he asks of me is meant to be done in his strength, not my own. I can't try to be godly. Godliness comes from his power working in me. It is a power I do not deserve and cannot manufacture.

NOW IT'S YOUR TURN

You have just seen how badly we're limited by laws and how badly you need God's strength. Now that you've seen how his amazing power can transform a person who waits on him, it's time to look at how to journey this road yourself.

Come along with me as we learn about the seven steps of finding lasting change in both your health and your relationships. The steps are laid out in a way that is simple to understand and simpler still to implement.

As Paul said, there are things to do and places to go!

What are you waiting for?

CHAPTER FIFTEEN

Seven Steps to Lifelong Victory

W hat you are about to read is the single greatest chapter I have ever written. Why? Because it contains the information many of you have been looking for your entire lives—the steps to lasting change by letting go of your own efforts and allowing God to work within you.

This is the chapter that may very well be the key to overcoming any battle that you are facing in life. Battles with poor eating habits or food addictions. Battles with relationships. Even battles with your faith.

Keep the connection, the cycle, in mind here. Remember that the cycle can be a positive one or a negative one.

If you make healthy choices, the results will be a greater likelihood of physical, emotional, and relational health. If you make unhealthy choices, you very likely will face physical, emotional, and relational distress. It seems that the choice is yours.

But many of you feel that making that choice is beyond your strength. And you are right. It is.

With that in mind, we look to the only source whose strength is greater than our own, the source that will allow us to stop the destructive cycle we may be trapped in currently and change it forever to one that is positive, one that will leave us healthier in all aspects of life.

The process of relying on God's strength can come in many ways. But the most direct way I have found is by implementing the following seven steps. In the remaining pages of this chapter we will examine the steps one at a time and give a few examples to help you understand how each step works in practical ways.

Seven Principles to Lifelong Victory

1. Identify your problem areas.
2. Admit your inadequacy.
3. Cry out to God.
4. Believe that God will rescue you.
5. Be willing to wait as long as it takes.
6. Expect God to give you a breakthrough.
7. Pray faithfully and persistently.

A PICTURE OF GOD'S PROVISION

When I need God to provide strength in areas in which I am weak, it helps me to think back on my life and remember times when his provision for me was unmistakable. A situation that happened in 1977 remains for me a striking picture of God's lavish love and provision.

Back then I owned an old Ford station wagon. I had no money. I was the assistant pastor of a church, and with our rent, food, insurance, and other expenses, Norma and I had no money for a different car. Besides, we didn't want to go into debt.

So I did what I do when I'm at the end of my resources: I prayed. In fact, my daughter, Kari, and I prayed every night, telling God we wanted to stay free from debt and asking that he provide us a car some other way.

Supernaturally.

We prayed that way every night for at least a year. I had total peace and confidence that God could do this. I knew he could do it.

So one day a wealthy friend of mine came to town, and we worked on a project together. When it was time for lunch, he said, "Let's just take your car. Give me the keys. I'll drive it." He sat down in the front seat, and immediately his body sprang forward toward the windshield. This wasn't a special feature, you understand. The springs were broken in that seat, and they launched the driver to the dashboard. I was embarrassed, to say the least.

"What's wrong with the seat?" he asked.

I told him I hadn't been able to fix the spring. When we arrived at the restaurant, my friend tried to open the back door, but it was rusted shut. "Is this your only car?" he asked, his mouth hanging open.

I told him it was.

He said, "This is pathetic."

"I couldn't agree with you more," I said. Then I patted the car and smiled good-naturedly. "Her days are numbered, so we're trying to enjoy her while we can." I never said anything to him or anyone else about what my daughter and I had been praying about every night.

My friend stared at me a minute, missing the humor in my comment. "Listen, Gary, go to any car lot after lunch and pick out whatever you want. I'll pay for it."

At that point, my mouth hung open. I was completely stunned. I had done nothing to deserve this opportunity; it had to be God's intervention. I knew all along that he could answer my prayer, I just didn't know how he would do it.

After a hurried lunch, I did what my friend suggested. I picked out a brand-new four-door Buick LeSabre. It was the first time in my life that I owned a new car.

I believe that all of this happened because I was willing to come to God empty-handed and ask for a miracle. Since then God has provided for me in countless ways, in material as well as spiritual matters.

The following seven principles outline the steps that prepare our hearts for approaching God and waiting for him to act in miraculous ways.

I'm excited for you because I know that God is going to use these steps to give you a breakthrough—a breakthrough beyond what you can imagine.

PRINCIPLE 1: IDENTIFY YOUR PROBLEM AREAS

Give all your worries and cares to God, for he cares about what happens to you.[1]

What problem areas are you dealing with? Because you have chosen to read this book, you probably are struggling with food and/or relationship problems. But you may be able to identify other areas as well—things you're hurting over, things you're discouraged or frustrated about, things you can't do anything about.

Maybe you are battling an addiction of some kind. Psychiatrist Gerald May, author of *Addiction and Grace*, lists numerous things we can become addicted to: eating, drinking, shopping, bad relationships, anger, approval, attractiveness, and power, to name a few.[2] He concludes that addictions result from weak relationships with God and people.

God has plans for your problem areas. Eventually he'll turn them into places of victory. But first you must identify these areas.

The best way to get an accurate view of your problem areas is to write them down. Be sure to actually do this; it's crucial at this stage of the process. I encourage you to keep a journal listing your addictions and problem areas. That way, you are aware of the situations you need to submit to God's power, and when he acts, you will see it clearly and be able to record what happens.

Here are a few points to remember as you identify your problem areas. The key is honesty. Scripture tells us to admit our sins and weaknesses. Don't be afraid to do this. We all have problem areas—lots of them. Be honest about your struggle points.

Spend time thinking about your list. Go through the possibilities at the beginning of this section again and see if you can find addictions or struggles you might have kept buried in your heart's closet until now.

For now, keep your list between you and God. No one else needs to know what you are admitting and what God may be trying to say to you. You might like to have someone pray with you about the list, even if that person doesn't know what's on the list. That can be a powerful source of strength.

Put your pen to the paper of your journal and begin. Leave absolutely nothing out.

PRINCIPLE 2: ADMIT YOUR INADEQUACY

"God opposes the proud but gives grace to the humble." Submit yourselves, then, to God. Resist the devil, and he will flee from you. Come near to God and he will come near to you.[3]

Once you have identified your problem areas, admit your inadequacy and humbly submit yourself and your problems to God. God promises to be gracious to those who are humble.

A humble person is simply a person who says, "I can't do this on my own. I am totally inadequate. God, I have to depend on you if anything is ever going to happen in my problem area." Of course, this attitude goes completely against our sinful nature and our culture, which screams at us to be self-centered and independent.

But not God. He asks us to be humble.

The passage in James reminds us we are to submit ourselves to God in humility, drawing close to him. We are to resist the devil—the forces that keep us bound to poor choices and addictions. When we do, their power over us will be broken.

One way to admit your inadequacy is to tell God you need him. Every day, as often as you think about it, admit your dependence on God. Say to him, "Okay, you're God, and I'm not. I need you! I'm out of control. I can't do this on my own."

Remember, when you draw near to God, he will draw near to you. That's a promise!

Confess your sins and weaknesses to God. Admit the ways you've strayed from his plan for your life. Remember, he already knows what they are, and his Son has already paid for all of them. Even the ones you can't admit yet.

This is not a time of guilt and condemnation but a time of regret and sorrow. The apostle Paul reminds us about the type of sorrow we're to have when we've sinned. "God can use sorrow in our lives to help us turn away from sin and seek salvation. We will never regret that kind of sorrow. But sorrow without repentance is the kind that results in death."[4]

You cannot save yourself. You cannot change yourself. It's okay to cry out to God. But while you will feel sad and grieve for a while, it won't last. "When you bow down before the Lord and admit your dependence on him, he will lift you up and give you honor."[5] Isn't that a great promise? He will lift you up.

As you humble yourself, remember that through Christ you have a whole new identity, as the following paraphrases indicate:

- You are made in God's image.
- You are a saint.
- You are God's work of art because he's living in you.
- You are righteous because of what Christ has done for you.
- You are fully accepted by God.[6]

Isn't that good news?

PRINCIPLE 3: CRY OUT TO GOD

Call upon me in the day of trouble; I will deliver you, and you will honor me.[7]

When you've identified your problem areas and humbled yourself enough to admit you cannot bring about change by yourself, you're ready for the next principle. You can take your troubles to God.

Throughout the Bible, the message is clear: If we cry out to God, he will help us.

Linda had identified her problem areas: She was thirty-seven, 125 pounds overweight, struggling to find any oneness in her marriage, and suffering from a host of physical ailments. The week before her class reunion, as she was searching her closet for something to wear to the big event, she was struck by a sense of failure. Linda was a former cheerleader who wore a size five in high school. None of her old friends would probably even recognize her.

She clenched her fists and gritted her teeth, furious with herself for not losing weight. "I hate you, Linda," she hissed at herself. Then the tears came. Hadn't she planned for this moment? Wasn't she going to lose weight the year leading up to the event and make the next twenty years a time of good health? Linda sighed and blinked back fresh tears. It didn't matter how many diets she had started over the past twelve months, she had failed every one.

"Okay, God," she whispered in the privacy of her closet. "I'm addicted to food and sugar and overeating."

Truthfully, Linda wasn't ready to cry out to the Lord. She was able to identify her problems, but she wasn't ready to submit her inadequacies to God.

Not yet. Not until the night of her reunion.

With dozens of classmates visiting near her table, Linda returned from the buffet line with her dinner plate, sat down, and immediately felt the chair buckle beneath her. Before she had time to catch herself, she fell to the floor as her plate flipped upside down and landed squarely on her stomach.

That night Linda admitted her inadequacies and cried out to God.

In the past I wouldn't have been able to relate to Linda's situation. But because God allowed me to suffer the problem area of overeating and excess weight, I've had a change of heart. I understand now that I don't want to operate in my own strength. I want to rest in God and cry out to him, admitting that I am at the end of my resources.

Although I never fully grasped God's grace and strength until recently, I definitely understood what it was to cry out to the Lord. It was something I had learned many, many years ago.

Before working in the area of marriage and family, I worked for the head of a large Christian organization. Although I felt I had done all I could to be a faithful worker, this man did something that deeply hurt me. It offended me and wounded my spirit. Although I severed ties with this man, the experience left me fearful and uncertain. I was no longer sure I could stay in the ministry.

I had tried everything I knew to rid myself of these feelings. I knew it was a problem area. I also knew that I could do nothing to change the situation; I was helpless.

One day I decided that I needed to be free from that fear and uncertainty. I went to my office, told my secretary that I didn't want anyone disturbing me all day, and shut the door. I spent three hours on my knees, truly crying out to the Lord. I remembered as many hurtful incidences as I could, and I literally spoke these words out loud with each memory: "[Name], I forgive you for [the offense]. Lord, I ask you to take away the hurt." When I was done, I was a basket case, a rag. I cried; I was emotionally spent and hungry.

Two weeks later I awoke feeling overwhelmed with love and forgiveness for this man. Needless to say, it never would have happened if I hadn't reached the end of myself and chosen to cry out to the Lord.

PRINCIPLE 4: BELIEVE THAT GOD WILL RESCUE YOU

Because of his great love for us, God, who is rich in mercy, made us alive with Christ even when we were dead in transgressions—it is by grace you have been saved.[8]

From this point on you no longer need to worry about whether you can save yourself from your problem areas. This Ephesians passage assures us that we are saved by God's grace, strength, and mercy, not by our own efforts.

Now it's time to believe this truth and apply it to your life.

In my personal journey to understanding the power and strength of God, I listed overeating as my problem area, humbled myself, and cried out to the Lord. But then I had to reach a point of believing that God would rescue me—really and completely believe this. It was something I had to do consciously every day.

Today, no matter what I struggle with, I believe that I can go to God and expect him to act. Two or three months after reading Rex Russell's book and after God's strength had freed me from my poor eating habits, I realized I could bring other areas to him and ask for his healing.

So I started making a list of other things I struggled with, other problem areas. During my adult life, I have occasionally battled with impure thoughts. (Guys, you know what I mean.) I understood that this was not something God wanted me to engage in. On some level I think I had resigned myself to believing that I would struggle in that area for the rest of my life. I had heard several Christian speakers say, "You'll never conquer that. You're a man, remember. This side of heaven, you'll always struggle with impure thoughts."

I had never heard anyone say, "God can free you if you cry out to him and trust him to release you."

Yet I think the Bible is pretty clear that God will give us the power to take our stand against any struggle. Look at what the apostle Paul says: "Be strong with the Lord's mighty power. Put on all of God's armor so that you will be able to stand firm against all strategies and tricks of the Devil. For we are not fighting against people made of flesh and blood, but against the evil rulers and authorities of the unseen world, against those mighty powers of darkness who rule this world, and against wicked spirits in the heavenly realms."[9]

I had to realize that I was fighting against external powers that we can't see, and they trip us up. I cried out to the Lord, "I know this isn't your will. I've read in your Word that you want my thoughts to be pure and wholesome. I admit that I struggle in this area and that I can't fight it on my own. I ask for your supernatural strength. I'm going to rest in you, just as I've done in my other problem areas, and watch you supernaturally do this work in my heart. I believe that you will rescue me from this struggle."

Have I found victory? Yes. And when I find myself back in the struggle, I do the same thing all over again. I identify the problem, humbly admit my inadequacy, cry out to God for help, and believe that he alone will rescue me.

The results have been miraculous for me, and I believe they'll be miraculous for you, too! Let's take a look at the next principle.

PRINCIPLE 5: BE WILLING TO WAIT AS LONG AS IT TAKES

I wait for the Lord, my soul waits, and in his word I put my hope. My soul waits for the Lord more than watchmen wait for the morning.[10]

God doesn't measure time in calendar pages and second hands. Scripture tells us that to the Lord a day is like a thousand years, and a thousand years like a day.[11] I'm not suggesting that your breakthrough will take a thousand years, but the truth is, it might feel as if it is.

That certainly has always been the case for me, and the secret is learning to enjoy the wait, to wait expectantly and not impatiently.

After I was hurt by that Christian leader I had worked for several decades ago, I cried out and prayed to God about my anger and desire for revenge for two years. Two years! Think about that. Every day and every night for two years I struggled with my anger and wondered when God was going to rescue me. I once heard that having bitterness and anger toward someone is like drinking rat poison and waiting for *the other person* to die. During those two years I felt exactly like that.

But one thing was always sure: I expected God to free me of my bitterness.

I was like the persistent widow in the New Testament; the judge finally answered her request because she kept pestering him, not letting him rest until he took care of her need.[12] I could almost hear God saying to me, "Because this Smalley guy keeps bothering me, I will see that he gets justice. He is wearing me out with his requests!"

I never doubted that God could release me from my bitterness because he had already answered my prayers so many times before. So I believed he would answer; it was simply a matter of waiting. I never got impatient with him.

The key was to believe God would work a miracle within me, granting me his supernatural strength. And then I had to be willing to wait until that miracle happened.

How long should you wait? As long as it takes. This is certainly true all through the Bible. Think of Abraham, who was promised descendants as numerous as the stars and still found himself childless when he was in his nineties. Or think about the Israelites, who wandered around the desert for forty years waiting for their entrance into the Promised Land. The stories of people who waited for their answers are plentiful.

When we wait for God to act, he gives us his supernatural strength. Listen to this word picture from the Old Testament: "Those who wait on the Lord will find new strength. They will fly high on wings like eagles. They will run and not grow weary. They will walk and not faint."[13]

And it's true. Abraham and the Israelites wound up soaring like eagles. Despite the fact that their waiting periods lasted years, even decades.

Part of the key here is having your focus on the right things during the waiting period. The Bible says to "wait on the Lord," and that's where our thoughts should be. When the problem area you're seeking deliverance from continually comes up in your mind, give it to God. This will make the waiting time peaceful and not a time of anxiety or impatience.

Here are some points to remember:

- Keep praying for God's help to conquer your problem area.
- Your breakthrough will almost always involve waiting on God's timing.
- Be willing to wait as long as it takes.
- Keep your focus on God and not on the problem area.

PRINCIPLE 6: EXPECT GOD TO GIVE YOU A BREAKTHROUGH

Now to him who is able to do immeasurably more than all we ask or imagine, according to his power that is at work within us, to him be glory in the church and in Christ Jesus throughout all generations, for ever and ever! Amen.[14]

Some of you may remember a song titled "Something Good Is Going to Happen." Well, that's exactly how I live. Whatever I'm praying for, I know it's going to happen soon.

Take a look at Amy's situation. She married Bill when the two were still in college; she was certain he was the man God intended for her. Bill was kind and generous, and Amy thought he would make the perfect husband and father. The fact that he didn't seem interested in attending church with her didn't seem like a big deal.

Three years after their wedding, Amy found herself crying out to God for help. "Father," she whispered, tears streaming down her face, "Bill's beginning to feel like an enemy. It's dividing our family and our home. Help me, God."

What happened to Amy was something that happens in many marriages. Her faith had created a chasm in her marriage. The results were pushing Amy to an emotional and physical breakdown. In the previous year she had gained twenty pounds and been diagnosed with an ulcer. A vivid picture, again, of how our relationships and health are intricately connected.

She wasn't asking Bill to become a Christian. She just wanted him to understand her need to take their two-year-old daughter to church each Sunday. But the issue had been a struggle from the beginning, and Amy came to the end of herself physically and emotionally.

In a sense Amy went through all the principles we've listed so far here.

She identified her problem area, humbly admitted her inadequacy to change her husband, cried out to God, believed he would help her, and was willing to wait.

Then she did something more: She began to expect a supernatural breakthrough. "I believed that God would find a miraculous way to change things in our lives," Amy says. "I believed it would be something obvious that would bring honor and glory to God, and it would happen soon."

Soon, of course, is a relative word. It may be today, it may be tomorrow, or it may be ten years from now. For one woman I know it was seven years before the breakthrough happened.

For Amy it was two years later. As Bill was driving home from work one night, he was broadsided in a major intersection. The impact sent his car spinning for fifty feet and wrapped it around a utility pole. Paramedics at the scene believed there was no way the person inside the vehicle had lived, but inside, Bill was very much alive. An air bag in his car had failed to engage, yet somehow he was virtually unharmed.

With his heart racing, Bill realized the peace and love and honor his wife had extended to him over the past two years. *What if God is real?* he asked himself in the minutes it took for paramedics to free him. Then the supernatural breakthrough happened. Suddenly Bill was overwhelmed with the presence of God.

After that there were no more questions, no doubts. That Sunday Bill was well enough to attend church with Amy and their daughter, and he hasn't stopped growing in his faith since.

Was Amy surprised? "Not at all," she says. "God is God. He was going to work something amazing and supernatural out of the situation with Bill. It was just a matter of what he was going to do and when he was going to do it."

God's Breakthroughs May Surprise You

If you're praying for an answer, make sure you're looking for one. For me, it almost always seems God brings about a supernatural breakthrough by giving me something to read. He'll have a pastor friend or a visitor or someone in my family hand me something I'm supposed to read. And through the message that particular article or book contains, God works to change my heart and bring about a breakthrough.

And God is able to do the same thing for you.

It's time to believe he will come through in some miraculous way with a conversation, an article, a Scripture passage, a book—maybe even this book. Believe that he is going to do it in such a way that it's going to be very evident it was his strength and power!

Breakthroughs Are Not Always without Setbacks

Sometimes, even after experiencing a breakthrough, problem areas can crop up again, and we can fail in an area from which we thought we were set free. God advises us to rejoice when we face struggles or temptations. When we rejoice, we return to the source of our joy. And this is exactly what we must do when problem areas return.

Let's say God frees you from your food addiction, and six months later you're at a party stuffing your face with cake and ice cream. The temptation is to go home and feel guilty. Relax! That's what you used to do. Now you can believe, as Paul says in Romans, that something good will come from your weakness. "I will boast all the more gladly about my weaknesses, so that Christ's power may rest on me. That is why, for Christ's sake, I delight in weaknesses, in insults, in hardships, in persecutions, in difficulties. For when I am weak, then I am strong."[15]

Don't burden yourself with guilt, which is unfruitful, or with fears of resuming your abuse of unhealthy foods. Focus only on God and his ability to free you from the problem you're facing again. His strength and power—the same power that dwells within you and delivered you from death when you became a believer in Christ—will deliver you again! Just relax and rest in him, and it will happen.

Remember what Scripture says about trouble: "Dear brothers and sisters, whenever trouble comes your way, let it be an opportunity for joy. For when your faith is tested, your endurance has a chance to grow. So let it grow, for when your endurance is fully developed, you will be strong in character and ready for anything."[16]

Wait for the Lord to act. Endure, and in the meantime, expect another breakthrough! Each time this happens in your life, you will see yourself closer to lasting change. Believe that you will wake up one day and realize that you are not controlled by that addiction, that habit, that problem area anymore. Months will go by without any struggle in that area, and you will have your confirmation. Because of God's strength, you will have a degree of victory and freedom that you've never known before. Handle setbacks the same way, expecting God to help you to grow past them.

That's what I mean by a supernatural breakthrough, and if it can happen once, it can happen again.

PRINCIPLE 7: PRAY FAITHFULLY AND PERSISTENTLY

For everyone who asks, receives. Everyone who seeks, finds. And the door is opened to everyone who knocks.[17]

When you ask God for freedom from your problem areas, the key is to be both faithful and persistent. As I pray for something in particular, I say, "Lord, it didn't happen last night or this morning, so I'll look for it to happen this afternoon. If it doesn't happen then, I'll keep praying for your answer and watching expectantly for it to take place. I will wait and rest in you and your timing."

Why should I be persistent and faithful in prayer? Because God says that if a human father can give good gifts to his children, how much more will God give strength and love and power to those who come to him day and night in prayer.[18]

Whenever the discussion turns to faithful and persistent prayer, it's important to remember a biblical truth: Before God will hear us, we need to take care of unfinished business. "When you are praying, first forgive anyone you are holding a grudge against, so that your Father in heaven will forgive your sins, too."[19]

Reconciled relationships not only increase our physical health, as we saw earlier, but they also help to make our prayer life more effective. The same principle is reiterated in the Old Testament, where the prophet Malachi warns the people that despite their weeping and wailing, God is not listening to their prayers. Why? Because the men have been disloyal to their wives.[20] These men broke the oneness we spoke of earlier in chapter 10.

Damaged relationships cause us emotional, physical, and spiritual harm. And one tangible proof is that unresolved wrongs and anger can stand as a barrier between us and God when we pray for a breakthrough.

Pray Faithfully

Let's take a look at what it means to pray faithfully. *Faith* is defined in the New Testament as "the confident assurance that what we hope for is going to happen. It is the evidence of things we cannot yet see."[21] In other words, you see it in your heart as you pray about it.

Praying faithfully also means praying without doubt. "I assure you that you can say to this mountain, 'May God lift you up and throw you into the sea,' and your command will be obeyed. All that's required is that you really believe and do not doubt in your heart. Listen to me! You can pray for anything, and if you believe, you will have it."[22]

Now, here's my interpretation of that passage. Let's say God lays it on your heart, through his Holy Spirit living inside you, that your problem area is going to be resolved through his power and strength—that a mountain of trouble in your life is going to be lifted up and thrown into the sea. It's your responsibility as a Christian to believe God can do it and to claim in faith that he will. You can tell people, "God has told me that a mountain is going to be lifted up and thrown into the sea." People may laugh, but remember, God wants us to believe we have received all that we ask for from him.

I balance that truth with the fact that I never pray for anything that isn't consistent with God's Word and that will not lead me to godliness. In other words, when he tells us we can ask for anything and we will have it, this applies when we are praying for his purposes to be accomplished, not our own.

Isn't that powerful?

Pray Persistently

Not only should we pray in faith, but we should also pray with persistence. A few pages ago I referred to the New Testament story of a persistent widow and a wicked judge.[23] The story indicates that the judge was callous, caring for neither God nor other people. A widow appealed to him for help because people were harming her. The judge ignored her for a while, but she was persistent. She came to him repeatedly asking for help, and eventually she wore out the judge. He determined to give her justice because she was grating on his nerves with her constant requests.

Jesus finishes the story by telling his listeners this: "Will not God bring about justice for his chosen ones, who cry out to him day and night? Will he keep putting them off? I tell you, he will see that they get justice, and quickly."[24] In other words when we persistently cry out to God day and night, he will give us justice. God is going to work in our lives. He's not a wicked judge. He loves us.

Jesus told another story to illustrate the importance of persistent prayer. Suppose you went to a friend's house at midnight, wanting to borrow three loaves of bread because a visitor had dropped in at your house and you had nothing to eat. At first your friend might call out from the bedroom, "Listen, don't bother me; the door is locked for the night, and we're all in bed. I can't help you this time." But if you keep knocking, eventually he'll get up and get you some food—not because of his friendship, but because of your boldness.[25]

Jesus finishes the story with these instructions: "And so I tell you, keep on asking, and you will be given what you ask for. Keep on looking, and you will find. Keep on knocking, and the door will be opened. For everyone who asks, receives. Everyone who seeks, finds. And the door is opened to everyone who knocks."[26]

I encourage you to take that promise seriously and personally. Keep on asking. Keep on crying out to God. Keep on praying faithfully and persistently.

You need God's strength and power to make changes you can never make on your own. Remember, his Holy Spirit is the only power strong enough to turn your problem areas into places of victory. And that's his will in the first place. He's the one who wants you to eat the healthy foods he has created. He's the one who wants you to have great relationships and freedom from cheap substitutes for love. It's his will. He gives his power freely.

Now it's time to ask for it.

CHAPTER SIXTEEN

The Amazing Connection

N ow that we're at the end of our journey, I can only imagine how excited you must be. You have hope and ideas and a way to seek God's power in your life like never before. Best of all, you have seen the amazing connection between food and love, and you know the cycles in a way you may never have understood before.

THE CYCLES

For too long we've looked at every other reason why people have unhealthy eating habits and unhealthy relationships. Here, now, we have finally been able to see the connection between food and love (SEE FIGURE 5).

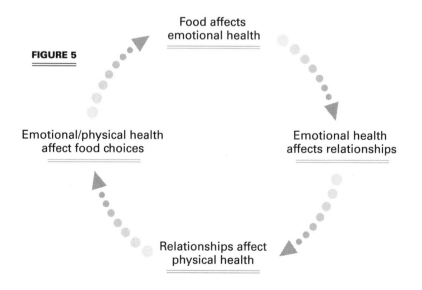

FIGURE 5

Food affects
emotional health

Emotional health
affects relationships

Relationships affect
physical health

Emotional/physical health
affect food choices

As we have seen, the cycle can be either a negative one or a positive one.

The Negative Cycle

The foods we choose to eat can either help or harm our self-image and emotional health. If we choose to eat unhealthy foods full of refined sugar, refined flour, hydrogenated and animal fats, and chemical preservatives, we will most likely find ourselves struggling with social isolation, irritability, mood swings, and even depression.

Our moods affect our relationships. When our emotional health is compromised, too often we find ourselves trapped in relationships that are weak or disintegrating.

Our relationships affect our physical health. Study after study shows a connection between weak relationships or social isolation and poor physical health.

Our emotional and physical health affect our food choices. When our relationships are poor and our overall health is poor, we will almost always feel unfulfilled and lonely. When this happens, too often we turn to cheap substitutes to find false love and satisfaction. We become capable of believing the lie that food is love.

The Positive Cycle

However, you can also find yourself in a positive cycle. How will that look?

As God grants you a breakthrough, it may show up in either your eating habits or your loving habits (relationship skills). Let's say he gives you the power to change your eating habits. Instead of eating processed foods, you nourish your body with healthy food choices. This, in turn, causes you to lose weight and plays a role in improving your self-image and your emotional health. With an improved emotional health, your relationships will also benefit, and you will find yourself much more easily resisting unhealthy foods.

The cycle holds true if God changes your relationship skills first. Once you learn to relate better to those around you—especially your spouse for those of you who are married—you'll feel better physically and emotionally. When this is the case, you'll be less likely to need unhealthy foods to provide yourself with false love and fulfillment, and you'll be more likely to eat healthy foods since eating will probably no longer be an emotional issue. As you nourish your body with healthier foods, you will find yourself with an improved self-image and better emotional health. And that, in turn, will foster the improvement God has given you in your relationships.

It's a positive cycle, and when operating in this way, the connection between food and love is a very good one, indeed.

LASTING CHANGE IS GOD'S WORK

Most of us struggle with problem areas either in the way we eat or the way we love and relate to others. Because of this, we need change. Some of us change for a while, but the change often doesn't last.

Lasting change comes only when we rely on God's strength for victory. We must learn to identify our problem areas, admit we can't change on our own, cry to God for help, and believe that he will rescue us. Then we wait expectantly for him to give us a breakthrough, believing and praying persistently and faithfully.

One of the significant aspects of lasting change that I have found as the result of the breakthroughs God has given me is a profound appreciation for how he turns my failures into victories. Some of the deepest lessons I have learned have come from the most difficult situations, whether those be problems with relationships or with food. God wants to give us "beauty for ashes, joy instead of mourning, praise instead of despair."[1] That's how he works. He turns hard times into good; he produces growth from painful pruning.

Today much of my life is a flourishing garden because of my problems with food and my problems with relationships, specifically the problem with that ministry leader. Nearly everything I do—my writing, speaking, and ministry—has come out of those kinds of problems. God turned them into a garden, a ministry to people who struggle—with marital issues, with family problems, with food problems. "[God] has made everything beautiful in its time."[2]

Do I understand what it is like to be powerless to do anything about my out-of-control eating? Yes! And now I have deeper compassion for people who struggle with addictive behavior.

Do I understand what it is like to be rejected and hurt and emotionally beat up and stomped on? Yes! And that's what many people face in their marriages and families. So I have compassion for people who struggle in their relationships. When I contacted that man who had hurt me, I thanked him for the way he treated me. I told him I was grateful because of what he had given me—the pain, the hurt, and the rejection. I told him that God had taken it and transformed me into a brand-new person as a result. The truth is this: God has taken my problem areas and past failures, and he has turned them into places of victory.

As you watch God give you beauty for the ashes of your past failures, remember this: When you give your life to Jesus, he frees you from guilt. "So now there is no condemnation for those who belong to Christ Jesus. For the power of the life-giving Spirit has freed you through Christ Jesus from the power of sin that leads to death."[3]

This is a crucial key to experiencing a breakthrough in God's power. Don't waste valuable time as well as spiritual and emotional energy feeling guilty because of your past failures. Don't get bogged down in areas that may prevent you from making progress in your problem areas—whether it's a problem with overeating or with a damaged relationship.

Of course, it is important to have reference points in past struggles. Otherwise you would never learn from them. But you must try to let go of burdens strapped to your backs—burdens God has already lifted from you.

FINALLY

Before you read the final two chapters of the book—"Special Concerns for the Single Person" and "Frequently Asked Questions"—I want to thank you for making the journey with me. It is my sincere prayer that God has touched you in some significant way through the pages of this book.

I am excited for you. I know that God will give you the breakthrough you have been anticipating. Enjoy your new freedom when it comes. Set your heart on the freedom Christ gives you. Once you experience that freedom, God will use you in powerful ways. I pray that your life, too, will be a garden that nurtures others, that reflects the goodness and power of God.

I leave you with this prayer:

I pray that from his glorious, unlimited resources he will give you mighty inner strength through his Holy Spirit. And I pray that Christ will be more and more at home in your hearts as you trust in him. May your roots go down deep into the soil of God's marvelous love. And may you have the power to understand, as all God's people should, how wide, how long, how high, and how deep his love really is. May you experience the love of Christ, though it is so great you will never fully understand it. Then you will be filled with the fullness of life and power that comes from God.

Now glory be to God! By his mighty power at work within us, he is able to accomplish infinitely more than we would ever dare to ask or hope. May he be given glory in the church and in Christ Jesus forever and ever through endless ages. Amen.[4]

ADDITIONAL ISSUES

CHAPTER SEVENTEEN

Special Concerns for the Single Person

M any unmarried people are caught in the negative cycle, eating the wrong foods as a way of medicating the loneliness of being single and then realizing poor emotional health, extra weight, and mood swings contribute to a poor self-image. For single people, it isn't a matter of learning to love someone correctly—especially when there seems to be no one to love.

How, then, can this terrible cycle be broken?

The answer is that everyone absolutely needs to be part of a relationship before healing can come. I know what you're saying. You're asking yourself how you can be part of a relationship when no one is knocking down your door or calling you for a weekend date.

Here's the catch: I'm not talking about a human relationship.

If you are ever to break free from the negative cycle you're in, you must first develop a deep and lasting relationship with your creator. As I mentioned before, God created all of us as relational beings. We simply will not be fulfilled and we cannot feel loved and nurtured without being part of a meaningful relationship.

And whether you're married or single, no relationship is more important than the one you need to share with God.

I'm certain that some of you reading this have thought yourself to be in a relationship with God, but you still struggle with a vast degree of loneliness and dissatisfaction. Others of you may never have considered a relationship with God. In either case, let's go over what a relationship with God looks like.

YOU AND GOD, THE PRIMARY RELATIONSHIP

I believe the most important relationship all people need to have is one with God. When nurtured, that relationship is one that will always be a benchmark for your other social interactions. The difference is that God will never change his mind or let you down. He will never have a bad day and take it out on you. He will never leave you or forsake you.[1]

God is steady in nature, never changing. "Jesus Christ is the same yesterday, today, and forever."[2] That's the best news of the day, if you're someone searching for love.

The very nature of a relationship is a two-way bond between two individuals. A relationship with God is no exception. I once counseled a man named Parker, who longed for a relationship with God. His question may sound something like yours. "I've always heard of people who can talk to God as if he's their best friend. But even though I've believed in God for a long time, I've never had that kind of relationship with him. What am I doing wrong?"

My answer to him is the same answer I would give you if you have that question. If you believe in God but don't feel close to him, ask him to draw closer to you. He will. He promises.[3]

A close relationship with God is different from a close relationship with a spouse or coworker. You can't call God on the phone or sit down and chat with him over tea. Or can you?

God desires a relationship that is every bit as close as that. The key is learning how to communicate with him throughout the day—not just when a crisis crops up. Our relationship with God should follow this diagram:

PRAYER = WE TALK TO GOD
BIBLE STUDY = GOD TALKS TO US

The more time we spend in prayer and Bible study, the closer our relationship with God will be. It's that simple. The benefits, though, seem to grow exponentially. In other words, during the first week of increased prayer and Bible study, you will begin to feel closer to God. But as the weeks continue, you'll begin to almost hear his voice even in routine situations throughout the day. You'll sense his presence more completely and feel his Spirit guiding you in the path you should go.

The stronger that bond grows—nurtured by prayer and Bible study—the closer and deeper that relationship with God will be. And for single people, having that type of relationship with God will fill holes you might otherwise fill with poor food choices. As you find real love and fulfillment in your relationship with God, you will find more strength from him and less need to reach for unhealthy foods.

As you change your food choices, you will experience physical and emotional benefits and almost certainly an improved self-image. When that's the case for you and when you no longer feel lonely because of your connection with God, you will be much more likely to make other social connections.

Let's take a look at some practical ways you can strengthen your relationship with God and change the negative cycle you may be caught in to a positive one where food and love are concerned.

PRACTICAL WAYS TO HAVE A BIBLE STUDY

Start your day with thirty minutes of Bible reading. Keep your Bible at your bedside, or move to a desk or table as soon as you wake up. If your schedule doesn't allow this morning time with God, wake up earlier, even if it means going to bed earlier.

Before you open your Bible, ask God to show you something special for the day, something that will help you better understand who he is and his plan for your life.

Find a Bible-study guide at a Christian bookstore, or simply make your way through the New Testament.

Read the Bible with an open notebook and a highlighter pen. This way you can mark up the text in your Bible, underlining and marking the Scripture passages that touch your heart, those in which God seems to be talking to you alone. I've never met a person who doesn't find these verses when reading the Bible with an open heart.

Read until you feel as if God has spoken to you, or read a predetermined amount of Scripture—such as two or three chapters. Then summarize in your notebook what you've read and how it applies to your life. Make sure to copy down the verse or couple of verses that particularly struck you as pertinent for that day and time in your life.

Finish the study with prayer, asking God to make his Word alive in your life that day. Be sure to thank him for his Word—your compass and handbook, your love letter from him. No matter what else changes, his Word will remain the same.

Remember, reading God's Word is a privilege, not a chore. It is not one more thing to check off your to-do list or a way of gaining favor with God. He loves you, regardless of whether you invest in your relationship with him. Bible study is merely a way to tap into a closer relationship with him. And by doing so, it is a way to fill the holes in your heart, holes you might otherwise be tempted to fill with wrong foods.

PRACTICAL WAYS TO DEVELOP A PRAYER LIFE

When you open your eyes in the morning, thank God for another day, and commit the next twenty-four hours to him. Marvel about what the day might hold, and go over your schedule with him. That early morning prayer might sound something like this: "Good morning, Lord. Thanks for a beautiful day, another day to talk to you and walk with you. My day is packed with business meetings and shopping errands, but I want to do them with you by my side. Help me to see you and hear you throughout the day. In Jesus' name, amen."

Then pray throughout the day. Try to think of new ways to thank God. Pray before you eat your meals, using your mealtime prayer as a way of examining what you're putting into your body. Is it something God created to improve your health? Or is it something that will work its way into the negative cycle we've been discussing in this book. Take your mealtime prayer seriously, and listen as God speaks to you about your food choices.

The Bible says to pray continuously. What does that mean? It means going through your daily routine with an awareness of his presence. How often should you talk to God throughout the day? As often as you can remember. I like to think of this as a running dialogue with God.

Remember that praying to God is not a mandate or a chore. It's not something God will grade you on. His love for you is unconditional and not based whatsoever on your ability to pray or the time you're willing to spend in communication with him. Rather prayer is an absolute privilege. It is your opportunity to release burdens and grow closer to the One who can fill the holes in your heart. In doing so you will undoubtedly develop a stronger sense of who you are in God's eyes. And that, in turn, will make you less likely to search out processed foods as a way of loving yourself and finding fulfillment in life.

IF EATING RIGHT AND LOVING RIGHT FEELS OVERWHELMING

My guess is that most of you agree with the material I've presented in this book so far. You can probably say, "I can see the connection between food and love. I understand that poor food choices will affect my emotions and that poor emotional health will affect my relationships. I believe fully that poor relationships will affect my physical health and that when my overall health is compromised, I'm much more likely to fill the holes in my life with poor food choices or even food addictions."

In fact, you might say, "Gary, I agree with every point you've made. There's just one thing I'm not clear on: *How am I supposed to change myself?*"

The answer is more simple than you may think. While some people might be able to make a rational decision and simply change their habits in eating and loving, most people will struggle. How are you supposed to change yourself?

You're not.

God will do the changing. All you have to do is take the issue to him and wait for his strength to give you the breakthrough you've been wanting both in eating right and loving right. Review the details of how to do that as they are outlined in chapter 15.

CHAPTER EIGHTEEN

Frequently Asked Questions

 s I have talked with conference participants about food and love, they often have questions about various issues. Maybe you have some, too. Let's see if we can address some of those questions here.

Is sugar really that bad for our bodies?

Yes, it is. During the past twenty years in the United States there has been an alarming increase in the intake of sugar—both among children and adults. At the same time there has been a 20 percent dramatic increase in the percentage of people who are obese or overweight. The most significant increase in obesity has been in children, half of whom will statistically remain obese throughout life.

In addition to being a direct cause of excess weight, this increase in sugar intake has also been significantly linked to the following disorders, listed by Calvin Ezrin, an endocrinologist and author of *Your Fat Can Make You Thin*.[1] The disorders marked by an asterisk (*) may be life-threatening or seriously life-altering.

- Diabetes*
- Pancreatitis*
- High blood pressure*
- Gallbladder disease*
- Some forms of cancer*
- Fatty livers*
- Snoring and sleep apnea*
- Proneness to accidents*
- Massive obesity*
- An increased risk of sudden death*

- Infertility
- Osteoarthritis
- Emotional changes

If you are a parent, a list like that should make you think twice about filling your precious children's lunches with sugary snacks or rewarding them with a soft drink after school. At the same time, most adults who have existed on a diet high in sugar must take note of the disorders listed above. Unless you reduce your sugar intake, you will most likely be headed toward one or more of them.

A list like that makes me cringe for the vast majority of us who consume high quantities of refined sugar. Look it over one more time. Sort of takes away the appeal of that morning doughnut or afternoon candy bar, doesn't it?

Gary, how did your family react to your new eating style?

When I first started changing my diet—and I had read all this information about how unhealthy it was to eat white flour, white sugar, and hydrogenated oils—I tended to be pretty frustrated with my family members for continuing to eat unhealthy foods.

The turning point came one night when our children and grandchildren joined us for a meal at a fifties diner. I was so irritated when I heard my adult children ordering poor foods for their own meals and similarly bad meals for my grandchildren, I thought, *How dare they feed these kids poison?* I was so upset that my facial expression and body language were communicating this to my family in a loud voice. I even said things like, "I can't believe you are feeding this poison to my grandkids, ruining their precious lives."

When I couldn't tolerate it any longer, I got up from the table, walked out of the restaurant, and ate my dinner outside.

Without a doubt, my actions were worse than what they were eating!

Really what I was doing was distancing myself from them, acting angry and rejected. I was isolating myself and isolating them. Remember the research on isolation? By alienating myself from them, I was doing more harm than if I had joined them for dessert. I was out of control. It was as if I couldn't get a handle on the fact that God hadn't brought this eating change about in their hearts yet.

I'm sure part of it was because my awareness of the damage unhealthy foods can do was new to me. That day at the restaurant I was simply overwhelmed with the feeling that everyone I loved had to get with the program. I wanted them to know everything I had discovered about health and nutrition.

That night after the diner experience, I was humbled and humiliated. I realized that I could no more force them to be healthy than they could have forced me to be healthy months earlier. The breakthrough in my life belonged completely to God, and if they were ever going to experience a similar realization, it wasn't going to come from me.

It's important to keep in mind that healthy food can cause a wedge in your relationships if it's something you flaunt in the faces of your loved ones. Remember the rule—extend grace, and let God do the changing.

What if my spouse doesn't want a food change?

If God has given you the breakthrough you've been waiting for and you're ready, in his strength, to change your eating habits, it's time to get excited. But what if your spouse isn't equally excited? What if he or she responds with one of these common reactions:

- You're always on some sort of food kick, aren't you?
- Don't tell me you're getting healthy on me.
- You can't expect me to give up my favorite foods just because you have a problem.
- Eat what you want, but don't force your new ideas on me.

Whatever you do, don't wield this book at your unwilling spouse as a weapon or tool of divisiveness. Don't imply that he or she is inferior for not being consumed with healthfulness. Don't suggest that your spouse is less enlightened. That's what I did that day in the restaurant, and I beg you not to make the same mistake.

Several books I read stated that changes in a person's diet and health are helpful even if they take years to implement. Remember, God will work on your spouse's heart in his perfect timing—not because you've been manipulating or making demands on him or her. You cannot change your spouse. You haven't been able to up until now, and you won't ever be able to.

That's God's job, so leave it to him.

What can I do to eat well and still eat with my family?

Here are some things you might do if your family resists your change:

- If you are the primary person in charge of cooking for the family, you could introduce a new, healthy meal once a week. But be careful. Don't start off with tofu, bean sprouts, and fish if your family is not accustomed to eating those foods. Try to serve familiar foods in more healthy ways.
- You could include more vegetables with meals the family already enjoys.
- Put fresh fruit around the kitchen so that it's available. Have a plate of apple slices out before dinner for snacking, or present a fruit bowl after dinner every few days in place of your normal desserts.
- Cook with olive oil, honey, and whole grains rather than hydrogenated oils, sugar, and white flour.
- Serve healthy foods in attractive ways. Accentuate the colors of fresh fruits and raw vegetables.
- My daughter, Kari, has begun juicing carrots, sweet potatoes, celery, and apples. Her four-year-old and seven-year-old, who typically don't like vegetables, are loving this new juice.

Most of all, remember that this is your breakthrough. It may one day be theirs also, but that will happen in God's timing. For now it is yours. With that in mind, you are responsible to provide yourself with healthy choices. And if you're the primary cook in the family, you're also responsible to maintain a sense of routine for your family and allow the changes to come slowly.

I want to eat healthy foods, but how can I do that with my busy schedule?

Many of you work forty to fifty hours a week and will have to let God help you figure out your own personal way of incorporating healthy foods into your regular routine. Here are some suggestions that might help:

- Plan your meals ahead.
- Take a lunch to work, and store it in the employee refrigerator if there is one. Otherwise invest in a thermal lunch box and an ice pack.

- Make dinners that will last for two nights instead of just one.
- Repeat your favorite healthy meals often. If you find something that works—fresh fruit and a chicken breast—for the lunch meal, have it often. This will save you time thinking up new ways to eat right.
- If you like variety, keep your home stocked with healthy choices.
- Be prepared. Instead of responding to the silent call of the vending machine at work when hunger overtakes you, bring an apple to work. That way you know right where to reach when the afternoon stretches out before you and hunger pains begin.

I've heard people say that it's very important to drink lots of water instead of other beverages. Is that true?

In doing research for this book, I ran across a theme that nearly every nutrition expert agreed on: Water is the cornerstone of good health. Why? Because water acts as a carrier service, shuttling nutrients throughout the body so that the entire body is fed. In other words, even if you eat healthy foods, the nutrients won't effectively make it to their numerous destinations if you aren't drinking enough water.

You need at least eight glasses per day in order for your body systems to function correctly. By the way, if you want to be extra kind to your body, drink purified, nonchlorinated spring water or distilled water.

Also, the best time to drink water is between meals. Fluid consumed during meals rushes food through the digestive system. This, then, washes away digestive juices including saliva, thereby interrupting digestion. Remember, don't get fanatical here and refuse water from the tap with lunch tomorrow. Just be aware of the health benefits of drinking the right water at the right time.

How important is exercise in maintaining normal weight?

I'm glad you asked that question. Wellness is multifaceted, and exercise is very important in maintaining overall health. Let me share eighteen reasons why I believe exercise is important.[2]

The following list is based on the benefits of thirty minutes of exercise, four times per week. Remember to check with your doctor before starting any exercise routine, especially if you have existing health problems. Exercise is beneficial because it:

1. Decreases heart disease by 50 percent and gives overall improvement in your cardiovascular system.
2. Helps strengthen the immune system and prevents diseases such as cancer, diabetes, and osteoporosis.
3. Lowers blood pressure and cholesterol levels.
4. Dramatically improves oxygen delivery to muscle cells.
5. Decreases mental anxiety and depression.
6. Increases energy, toned muscles, and weight loss.
7. Relieves stress by releasing tranquilizing endorphins.
8. Changes the brain and nerve cells into energy, producing more energy than the body uses.
9. Aids digestion, strengthens muscles and bones.
10. Helps all glands function more efficiently.
11. Delays the onset of fatigue.
12. Prevents muscle deterioration.
13. Increases muscle flexibility and range of motion.
14. Lessens chance of injury.
15. Enhances posture.
16. Raises HDL (the body's good cholesterol).
17. Promotes a more restful sleep.
18. Makes for a longer life with improved quality of life as well.

What I learned right away when I began to exercise several decades ago is that I didn't like to exercise just for the sake of exercising. Whether I ran or walked, I would be bored in ten minutes. In fact, even now I find that for the first mile or first ten minutes of exercising, I dislike it as much as anything in my life. But after ten minutes, my body systems kick in and send me a little message. Something like, "Hey, we like this. Keep it up."

Even though I don't really enjoy exercising, I do it almost every day.

For nearly twenty years I exercised by jogging long distances. I even ran in one marathon. But today I agree with health experts such as Andrew Weil, the sponsors of the Pritikin Diet, and experts at the Cooper Clinic at the Cooper Aerobics Center in Dallas. They now believe that moderate walking is better than running.

My exercise life evolved after that, and I began using that time as a meeting place with God. For years, while I ran and walked, I would pray. An hour would pass, and I would be fired up because I spent the whole time with God, sharing with him the desires of my heart, reflecting on his Word.

When I was busy thinking about God, I wouldn't have to think about running or walking.

Today, the reason I actually enjoy exercising is that I always do something else at the same time. I use a treadmill and read books. Some people can't do that, but I encourage you to find the exercise that you can enjoy or combine with some other enjoyable activity such as reading, watching TV, knitting, or doing some hobby.

Sometimes getting exercise is as simple as going up and down your stairs several times a day or parking your car farther away from your office, the grocery store, or wherever, and walking a few blocks. Just look for some practical and creative ways to make this a reality in your life.

My friend exercises with her husband. Would exercise really help my relationship with my husband? If so, what are some ways we could get fit together?

The next key to enjoying exercise is involving your spouse or a close friend. Shared fitness activities can be a source of laughter, love, and light in your relationships. Exercising can be a time when conversations are deep and uncluttered by the sameness of everyday life. Take a look at the following list, and see if you can incorporate any of these into your relationships:

1. Walk together. Thirty minutes or an hour will pass quickly if you are in conversation. The health benefits are multiplied because you took time to do this together, and your marriage or other relationship will experience a boost in the process.
2. Bike together. This is something that can be done in your neighborhood or at a park or on a mountain trail. I know a woman who used to take her husband on surprise mountain-bike rides, complete with a backpack dinner to share at some scenic site. The benefits of this type of shared fitness activity are numerous.
3. Join a health club together. Instead of spending your evenings in front of the television, get active together. If you don't care for the club scene, purchase some simple equipment or an exercise video, and actually use it together.
4. Take ballroom dancing lessons once a week.
5. Join a local park softball team.
6. Play tennis at a local high school.
7. Get a book on local hiking trails, and discover a new trail every month.

8. Put up a basketball hoop on the garage, or buy a portable hoop and spend a half hour playing one-on-one or H-O-R-S-E together.
9. Get a Ping-Pong table, and have tournaments between the two of you.
10. Go jogging at a local school track, and work together to build your distance and stamina.

Just writing that list makes me smile with the possibilities. If it sounds fun to you, take the list to your spouse or friend.

Remember that if you avoid exercise, you run the risk of health problems. A sedentary lifestyle will contribute to major illness as surely as wrong foods will. And we all know the toll that illnesses—especially serious illnesses and diseases such as cancer and diabetes—can take on a relationship. But even minor illnesses can affect our relationships and take us further and further from a state of wellness.

How does the food-love connection affect relationships other than marriage?

When the connection between food and love leaves us trapped in the negative cycle, other relationships will be affected as well. Children, teens, and single people are also subject to poor relationships if they get caught in this cycle. The following is a list of relationships that might be affected:

CHILDREN. Children's emotions are affected by the food they eat. When bad food choices lead to emotional disequilibrium, conflict and isolation are not far around the corner. It is crucial for children to avoid this area of emotional struggle, especially in their relationships with us, their parents. What can you as a parent do to help your children, who may be struggling with isolation and a poor self-image? Try feeding them a diet of healthy foods for two weeks, and see if there's a difference. Again think of the students each year diagnosed with ADD or ADHD. True, hyperactivity can be caused by a chemical imbalance in the brain, and on occasions it definitely requires medication. But many doctors will tell you the success they've had treating hyperactive children by altering their food choices.

TEENS. Hormones are already raging and can cause unsettling feelings for teens. For many people the decision to reach for unhealthy foods as a way of giving themselves artificial love and comfort begins in the teenage years. Teens who make that choice will often pay the price in excess weight and a poor complexion, two physical traits that can be devastating to a teenager's emotional health. Relationships with peers are especially important during these years, and teens with a healthy view of themselves and their place in society will generally gravitate toward healthy relationships. Likewise, teens who struggle emotionally may gravitate toward others like themselves. Once a teen has fallen into the pit of a poor self-image or social isolation, other problems such as drug use, rebellion, and suicide may not be far behind. Hear me on this: I am not saying that poor eating habits will lead to suicide. What I am saying is that the connection between food and love can lead to conflict and isolation for teens. Because this is already a difficult period of adjustment, it's especially important to keep a close eye on your teenager's emotional health. Again, it's certainly worth exploring whether a dietary improvement might help your teen to feel stronger emotionally.

COWORKERS. Anyone who has ever held a job knows how crucial it is to maintain a healthy relationship with both coworkers and the person in charge. Nearly every person who is fired from a job had difficulty relating to either a boss or a coworker. When the connection between food and love leaves a person feeling isolated or in conflict with others (bad moods, uncontrolled anger, etc.), it will very often affect life in the workplace as well. As with other relationships, there may be a number of factors that make a workplace unbearable. But if you seem unable to get along with a boss or coworkers, consider whether you might eliminate certain processed foods or caffeine for a period of two weeks. Is it possible that your diet may be contributing to your short fuse? Could it be that a healthier diet will make life in the workplace more bearable, even if it doesn't change your circumstances? Do the two-week experiment, and see for yourself whether you feel more stable and relaxed, more tolerant of the difficulties at work and the difficult people you may work with.

What are the overall benefits of integrating eating well and loving well?
Here are a few benefits for starters:

209

- When you focus on healthy living, you will release tension, thereby improving your health.
- As your health improves, you will have more energy to love the people in your lives, especially your family.
- You'll get sick less often. Since I started eating right a few years ago, I've not had any colds, flu, or headaches. That overall health improves my relationship with Norma and the rest of my family.
- The physical love between a husband and wife or the appropriate physical touch in other important relationships will cause a sense of well-being and help ward against disease.
- The healthier you feel, the more focused you'll be on your relationship with God.
- A strong relationship with God will allow his strength to change the problem areas in your life and will greatly reduce the need for cheap substitutes.

Can foods cure illnesses?

In *What the Bible Says about Healthy Living,* Rex Russell cites a study done by Dr. Michael Wargovich of Anderson Hospital in Houston, Texas. This research shows that scientists are looking at several isolated chemicals that seek to stop cancer from developing even when a carcinogen is present.

Wargovich reports, "In the last three to four years, we found that fruits and vegetables contain a variety of powerful chemicals which interact and bind to chemical carcinogens rendering them inactive. Some of these chemicals might also interfere with the metabolism of carcinogens in the liver."[3]

While I was researching for this book, I learned about a pastor who all his life ate the standard American diet and developed cancer twenty years ago. He decided not to use drugs or chemotherapy but instead to eat only raw vegetables, raw fruits, nuts, and grains. His cancer was cured, and he hasn't had any illnesses, even a common cold, in more than nineteen years.

Many doctors believe that some muscle pains and arthritic conditions can be reduced or eliminated with dietary changes. Toxic buildup of waste products in the muscles greatly inhibits the proper function of the muscular system and not only leads to inflammation and pain but also weakens our immune system.

Can foods cause illnesses?

The truth is, many foods have lost too much of their original value and therefore are not only failing to nourish our bodies but also adding toxins that weaken and lower our immune systems. Consequently, many Americans are suffering from minor illnesses like colds, flu, and headaches as well as major illnesses such as heart failure, a variety of cancers, diabetes, and many other forms of immune disorders.

I experienced a direct relationship between the foods I ate and various physical symptoms. In one case the problem was right under my nose. Actually, at first the problem was *in* it.

All my life I have had major sinus headaches. On the bad days nauseating headaches would start early in the morning. I would be so sick I couldn't eat anything. Then I would have the dry heaves around noon, and I would vomit for several hours—not a good thing to be doing with a throbbing headache.

I knew that my headaches were affecting my marriage because I didn't want to see my wife when I was sick as a dog and throwing up. And why would she want to see me? I was grouchy and irritable.

After researching about the power of food, one of the first things I found out is that processed milk and cheese sometimes caused a person to excrete excess mucous. Could it be that my consumption of cheese and milk was leading to my sinus headaches? Could it be that these foods were why I was rarely able to breathe clearly through my nose? There was only one way to find out.

I cut out milk products, and I am happy to say that I've never felt better! It's miraculous, really. Even as I write this, I can breathe through my nose! It's amazing.

In 1980 I had six major physical ailments, and my doctor said that the food I was eating was contributing to each one of them. He encouraged me to start eating the way I'm encouraging you to eat today. I had never understood the impact of food on my body. When I read about health food, I just thought it was a strange way that only weird people ate. I didn't think I could do it, so I never really tried. As a result, my limited efforts never made an impact on me.

How do you eat? What do you try to eat every day?

Ever since I've experienced my breakthrough in the area of overeating and understanding the relationship between food and love, people have been asking what my lifestyle actually looks like. Of course, not everyone will make the same changes I did. But this has worked for me. For that reason, I thought I would give you a picture of an average day now that, through God's power, my health habits have changed for the better.

I realize I have a different schedule from many of you. Sometimes it's crazy for forty-eight hours straight; other times it's more like that of a retired person. Anyway, here's a typical day for me when I am at home, not traveling to speak at conferences.

Before I describe what I eat, I want to say that my whole attitude about food has changed in the past few years. I see food as fuel to feed my ever-changing cells and to keep my immune system strong. I am no longer concerned about how food looks, tastes, or smells. I have come to love—and sometimes crave—foods that did not appeal to me several years ago because I was trying to satisfy only my taste buds and not my body's real needs. My taste buds have changed so much that I really enjoy fresh foods and many natural drinks.

First thing in the morning, I drink four to six glasses of distilled water. Next, I mix eight ounces of raw juices with soy milk (dairy products affected my sinuses and gave me headaches, but certain dairy alternatives work for me) and green barley powder. I drink that down and actually love it now. I make juice from a variety of vegetables and fruits. I usually juice four medium carrots, two stalks of celery, two inches of medium sweet potato, half of a medium beet, some spinach leaves, and one apple. Sometimes I add broccoli and other vegetables.

Next, I usually exercise on the treadmill for thirty to sixty minutes, pray and fellowship with the Lord, read and/or write. Sometimes I just walk outside for an hour.

For breakfast, I might have beans and a multigrain cereal with raw honey. I have two jars of honey, one with a honeycomb and one without. I almost always include oats or oat bran in my cereal mix. I know that high-fiber cereal blocks a lot of the fat and cholesterol that I don't need to have in my body.

Then I have vanilla oat milk or soy milk and bread that I have baked. I use a spread called Take Control instead of butter; it's similar to regular margarine, but without the hydrogenated oils. Take Control includes a substance that actually can reduce your cholesterol level by 20 to 30 percent. I've been using that for about six months, and again, I've learned to love it.

I graze throughout the day on cooked fish, chicken, nuts, fruits, seeds, and unprocessed cheese (You can order this wonderful cheese from Morningside Dairy, 417-469-3817).

For lunch, I may have salmon, chicken, or a small can of chunky white tuna. I put the tuna in a strainer and run hot water over it to get out as much salt as possible. Then I press the water out of it. And I use a new, unprocessed mayonnaise—Canola Mayo—that I buy in my grocery store. I don't use any salt. Sometimes, I add chopped grapes, celery, or carrots to the tuna before I put it on my bread. I'll eat that with a glass of oat milk. Once in a while I have whole baked potato chips or corn chips with no hydrogenated oils in them. I find these chips in my grocery store, right on the shelf next to the chips that are loaded with fat and chemicals.

Then, for dinner I often steam vegetables, or stir-fry them in olive oil, and eat them with brown rice. I usually have a few pieces of bread with Take Control margarine. Norma and I sometimes have chicken, fish, steak, beans, or baked potatoes.

I drink ten glasses of water before three o'clock in the afternoon. However, I don't drink any water after. At my age, I'll be up twice during the night if I start drinking water late in the afternoon or in the evening.

Each of you should discover what your body needs. Try to find a medical person who is also a nutrition expert. This person can give you the most reliable instruction and direction. In addition to that, read books by reputable authors, and take charge of the fuel you put into your body.

If you would like to know more about my specific recipes or food choices and how they've become part of my daily life, let me know by contacting me at **www.smalleyonline.com** or **www.Tyndale.com** and following the links to the Gary Smalley survey.

How can I make whole grains part of my daily life?

Whole grains still have the germ intact and are, therefore, considered "living" foods, foods your cells need. Whole grains include whole oat kernels, oats, wheat germ, wheat, and a dozen other grains you can buy from most health food stores. I like to buy them whole and put them in my blender, break them up, and make cereal out of them in the morning or put them into different foods.

Since the germ of the grain will go bad quickly, most commercial bread mills remove the germ—even on products labeled "whole wheat" or "whole grain." One way to assure optimal benefits from these whole grain breads is to add the wheat germ back in as part of the sandwich contents. For instance, sprinkle a tablespoon of wheat germ over the peanut butter.

Suggested Reading List

 n addition to giving you a list of some of the books I've read on my journey to health, let me give you a summary of some of the very good books and programs about nutrition and weight loss.

SYNOPSES OF WEIGHT-LOSS AND NUTRITION BOOKS

The PRISM Weight Loss Program by Karen Kingsbury and Toni Vogt (Sisters, Ore.: Multnomah, 1999).

> The book outlines the PRISM weight-loss program, a strong, nutrition-based weight-loss program. It deals with treating problem eating from all three angles: physical, emotional, and spiritual—the same three we've been talking about in the chapters of this book. PRISM also involves the small-group concept, which I think is so important. However, if small groups aren't your thing, PRISM is available for individuals as well.
>
> Basically the concept is to cut out white sugar, white flour, and processed foods. At the same time, PRISM leaders encourage a calorie limit and ask participants to avoid weighing themselves. They ask participants to sign a contract that they won't eat unhealthy foods, and if they do, they call one of the people in the small group, confess, and have the person pray with them.
>
> Visit the PRISM Web site at **www.pwlp.com.**

Food Smart! by Cheryl Townsley (Colorado Springs, Colo.: Piñon Press, 1994).

> This sound book advocates giving up caffeine, alcohol, foods containing preservatives, additives, chemicals, high-sodium products, MSG, food coloring, refined sugar, white flour, all products that contain margarine or hydrogenated oils, white rice, carbonated beverages, salt-cured or smoked foods, and foods that contain nitrates.
>
> Townsley insists that there are no "normal physical complaints" and that headaches, acid indigestion, and other common ailments are all

signs that the body is in some sort of distress. It's a phenomenal book. You'll also find it very helpful concerning how foods affect relationships.

The Zone by Barry Sears with Bill Lawren
(New York: Regan, 1995).

The Zone has been around for several years and is still wildly popular. It involves a fairly simple matter of combining the macronutrients (protein, carbohydrates, and fats) at every meal for optimal energy and body performance. I am aware of many people who have lost weight and gained health on this program.

Like other successful plans, *The Zone* suggests that no sugar or processed foods be eaten. However, if they are, it asks participants to get immediately back onto the plan. This plan teaches that you are never more than one meal away from living in the zone.

The Pritikin Weight Loss Breakthrough: Five Easy Steps to Outsmart Your Fat Instinct by Robert Pritikin
(New York: Dutton, 1998).

The Pritikin program, which has been successful for years, advocates eating these foods: a wide variety of leafy, stalk, and root vegetables; beans (including zooky beans, black beans, black-eyed peas, etc.); a wide variety of fresh fruits; all grains, including barley, brown rice, buckwheat, corn; low-fat animal foods (limited to three ounces per day), including fish, white-meat chicken, turkey, lean beef, egg whites, skim milk, etc.; herbs, spices, sauces, and dressings.

In addition, the program encourages several healthy habits: walk at least two miles a day, a minimum of thirty minutes at least four times a week; eat twelve small meals a day; expose yourself to twenty minutes of sunlight a day for vitamin D; drink eight to ten glasses of water per day.

Robert Pritikin says people become overweight and develop disease because they eat too much fat, causing lipotoxemia, which he claims leads to a wide array of diseases.

Weight Watchers Diet Plan.

I went to Weight Watchers for months a few years ago, and I like the way they encourage you to eat. What they don't really emphasize enough is the importance of avoiding white flour, sugar, and hydrogenated oil. So if you avoid the unhealthy foods discussed in this book, you will do fine in this program. The beauty of Weight Watchers is that you are in a group, being supported by others, sharing with them how you're doing. Your leader is encouraging you, and you gain so much strength from that!

Eight Weeks to Optimum Health by Andrew Weil
(New York: A. A. Knopf and Random House, 1997).

This national best-selling book is extremely helpful. Dr. Weil's approach is very honoring, nonthreatening, and gracious. He gives specific ways to eat a healthy diet, including food supplements and herbs that he has found to be very healthy. There are certain tonics that he uses, and he talks about those in detail here. Basically, his program sticks to healthy, God-given foods the way other programs do. But it does a better job than some books of explaining the health benefits of those foods.

Eat More, Weigh Less by Dean Ornish
(New York: Quill, 2001).

Dean Ornish is the doctor who totally reversed heart disease six months after beginning this diet. Ornish insists that you avoid all meat, including chicken and fish. Avoid all oils and oil-containing products, including margarine and most salad dressings. Avoid avocados, olives, nuts and seeds, high-fat or low-fat dairy products (including whole milk, yogurt, butter, cheese, egg whites, cream, etc.). Avoid sugar, simple sugar derivatives, honey, molasses, corn syrup, high-fructose syrup, and the like.

One word of caution about this diet: Many experts disagree with the idea of eliminating all fats. God-given fats such as nuts, grains, avocados, and olives have been linked to increased longevity and have been shown to cause a reduction in leukemia and cardiac arrhythmias. However, there are situations when the elimination of all fats may be life-saving. Be sure to check with your doctor before beginning this or any health or diet plan.

BOOKS
(Books marked with an asterisk were particularly helpful to me.)

Anderson, Neil T. *The Bondage Breaker.* Eugene, Ore.: Harvest House, 2000.

Astor, Stephen. *Hidden Food Allergies.* Garden City Park, N.Y.: Avery Publishing Group, 1988.

Barnard, Neal D. *Foods That Fight Pain.* New York: Harmony Books, 1998.

Barnes, Emilie, and Sue Gregg. *The 15-Minute Meal Planner.* Eugene, Ore.: Harvest House, 1994.

Bellerson, Karen J. *The Complete and Up-to-Date Fat Book: A Guide to the Fat, Calories, and Fat Percentage in Your Food.* Garden City Park, N.Y.: Avery Publishing Group, 2001.

Brand-Miller, Jennie, et al. *The Glucose Revolution.* New York: Marlowe and Company, 1999.

*Broer, Ted. *Maximum Energy.* Lake Mary, Fla.: Creation House, 1999.

Cooper, Kenneth H. *Advanced Nutritional Therapies.* Nashville: Nelson, 1996.

*_____ . *Controlling Cholesterol the Natural Way.* New York: Bantam Books, 1999.

Eades, Michael R., and Mary Dan Eades. *Protein Power.* New York: Bantam, 1996.

Fairechild, Diana. *Jet Smart.* Maui, Hawaii: Flyana Rhyme, 1992.

Gould, K. Lance. *Heal Your Heart.* Piscataway, N.J.: Rutgers University Press, 1998.

Herzog, Greg, and Craig Masback. *The 15-Minute Executive Stress-Relief Program.* New York: Perigee, 1992.

*Jampolsky, Gerald G., and Diane V. Cirincione. *Love Is the Answer.* New York: Bantam, 1990.

*Jantz, Gregory L. *Hope, Help, and Healing for Eating Disorders.* Wheaton, Ill.: Harold Shaw, 1995.

Katz, Lawrence C. *Keep Your Brain Alive.* New York: Workman Publishing, 1999.

Kowalski, Robert E. *8 Steps to a Healthy Heart.* New York: Warner Books, 1992.

Kuhn, Cynthia, Scott Swartzwelder, and Wilkie Wilson. *Buzzed.* New York: W. W. Norton, 1998.

Kuzma, Jan W., and Cecil Murphey. *Live 10 Healthy Years Longer.* Nashville: Word, 2000.

Loritts, Crawford W. Jr. *Make It Home before Dark.* Chicago: Moody Press, 2000.

Markman, Howard, Scott Stanley, and Susan L. Blumberg. *Fighting for Your Marriage.* San Francisco: Jossey-Bass, 1994.

*May, Gerald G. *Addiction and Grace.* San Francisco: HarperSanFrancisco, 1991.

*McMillen, S. I., and David E. Stern. *None of These Diseases.* Grand Rapids: Revell, 2000.

*McVey, Steve. *Grace Rules.* Eugene, Ore.: Harvest House, 1998.

*———. *Grace Walk.* Eugene, Ore.: Harvest House, 1995.

*———. *Living with the King of Kings in Grace Land.* Eugene, Ore.: Harvest House, 2001.

Murray, Michael T. *Heart Disease and High Blood Pressure.* Rocklin, Calif.: Prima, 1997.

Rona, Zoltan P. *Childhood Illness and the Allergy Connection.* Rocklin, Calif.: Prima, 1997.

Roth, Geneen. *Breaking Free from Compulsive Eating.* New York: Plume, 1993.

*Russell, Rex. *What the Bible Says about Healthy Living.* Ventura, Calif.: Regal, 1996.

Shamblin, Gwen. *The Weigh Down Diet.* New York: Doubleday, 1997.

Sheps, Sheldon G., ed. *Mayo Clinic on High Blood Pressure.* Rochester, Minn.: Mayo Clinic, 1999.

Simone, Charles B. *Cancer and Nutrition.* Garden City Park, N.Y.: Avery Publishing Group, 1992.

Smalley, Gary, and John Trent. *The Two Sides of Love.* Wheaton, Ill.: Tyndale House, 1990.

Stanley, Scott, et al. *A Lasting Promise.* San Francisco: Jossey-Bass, 1998.

*Steward, H. Leighton, et al. *Sugar Busters!* New York: Ballantine, 1998.

Swindoll, Charles R. *The Grace Awakening.* Dallas: Word, 1992.

Swope, Mary Ruth. *Green Leaves of Barley.* St. Louis: Swope Enterprises, 1998.

*Whitaker, Julian. *Dr. Whitaker's Guide to Natural Healing.* Rocklin, Calif.: Prima, 1996.

ARTICLES, BOOKLETS, AND TAPES

Health Alert Publications. Monterey, Calif.: Health Alert Publishers, 2000. Phone: 800-231-8063.
  Today's Most Promising Health Breakthroughs

The Secret Link between Indigestion and Disease
How to Cure "Incurable" Pain
Healing Heart Program
Cures That Kill . . . Cures That Heal
Lin, Judith. *How Food Affects Your Mood, and How to Change Your Life!* (Boca Raton, Fla.: American Media Mini-Mags., Inc., 2000)
McVey, Steve. *The Garments of Grace* (tape series). Atlanta: Grace Walk Ministries (to order, call 1-800-472-2311).
Schulze, Richard. *Dr. Richard Schulze's Patient Handbook.* School of Natural Healing, 1995.
"Pie in the Sky Diet Promises Spur Concerns on Safety," *The Atlanta Journal-Constitution*, 29 October 2000.
Sullivan, Andrew. "Why Do Men Act the Way They Do?" *New York Times Magazine*, reprinted in *Reader's Digest* (September 2000): 82.

Survey Results
from Smalley Seminars

A s I mentioned in previous chapters, I've had the opportunity to survey 20,000 couples as to the amazing connection between food and love. I've sprinkled some of those results in the book, but I wanted to share the rest with you here. I believe the overall message suggests a great need among married people to find answers and hope in areas of eating, relating, and God's power to find victory in both areas.

These questions deal particularly with physical health and God's power to bring lasting change, but the connection to the marriages of these people is quite clear. Read on, and see if you agree.

QUESTION: *Have you experienced God's power and grace as it relates to weight loss or addiction?*

- There is so much freedom in listening to my body tell me what to eat instead of focusing on what the world tells me to eat or not to eat. My biggest addiction was people-pleasing instead of God-pleasing. I am being freed from this every day by using the Christian principles of relying on God's power.
- I feel the weight I lost blessed my life in many ways. Without discipline from God, I could not have done it.
- Before I became a Christian, I was a professional, but I also used drugs and spent a lot of time at parties. God's grace allowed me not only to leave it all behind but also to dislike the lifestyle I had been leading.
- I was very addicted to caffeine and had to take myself off it because I got fibrocystic disease. With my husband and mostly with God's help I have been very successful.
- I am praying and trying. I am forty-one and have never until now had a weight problem. I am finding the more comfortable I am with my spouse, the less stressed out I am and the easier it is to overeat. I am now twenty pounds overweight.
- God took away my desire, need, want, and taste for dessert. Especially chocolate. Now I eat fruit instead, and rich desserts only once a week instead of three times a day.

- I believe God has given me the self-discipline it takes to watch what I eat and keep my weight at the desirable level for my health. After having four children, it is important to me to be as attractive to my husband as I can be.
- I constantly remind myself that I am a caretaker of the temple of God and I have been called to maintain it the best way possible.
- It is effective to combine Bible study with weight loss.
- I learned through Bible study and prayer that my self-image as it relates to weight and appearance is not dependent on Hollywood standards. The most important thing I have learned and the most motivating factor was that my body is the temple of the Holy Spirit and that God's desire for me is that I treat it with honor and respect and not defile it with food-related or other addictions.
- When I fail today and remind myself of past failures, God helps me see tomorrow.
- Three years ago I was approximately ninety pounds overweight. I prayed and prayed for God to help me lose weight because I had tried every diet. I would lose ten pounds and gain twenty. I realized the value of exercise and began to actually enjoy walking and working out. I lost almost sixty pounds in about seven months.
- I do everything in moderation and go to God, not food, for comfort.
- You must substitute something positive for something negative—replace overeating with reading God's Word.
- God instantly delivered me from smoking, and it has been almost a year since my last puff. I know he can deliver me of my food challenges. I just have to get out of his way and let him take over.

QUESTION: *If certain foods have been proven to lower your immune system, increase your risk of diabetes, heart failure, cancer, and other diseases, what type of information would you need to change your eating habits?*

- Facts and examples of real people who ate these foods and developed these diseases.
- Quick-and-easy recipes for the whole family on the go.
- List of what foods help and which hurt.
- Substitutions for the foods you like. Nobody wants to lower pleasure in eating by eating healthy foods. If you can find a way to eat healthy without sacrificing taste, people will do it.
- Scientific data.

- I need support and my husband to be involved with me—not just as a participant where I do all the work, but as a coworker.
- The scriptural perspective of food, eating foods closer to the way God made them—fresh and unrefined.
- Eating high-fat foods several days in a row causes me stomach pain. I enjoy life more when I do not overeat. I would like more information on how much God wants us to eat.
- I need to know how to not crave sweets.
- More specifics of how daily life is affected by good and bad choices. How to make healthy foods taste good.
- I would need to know which foods and combinations of foods will boost my immune system and lessen my susceptibility to disease. I would also need things to do or eat that are very quick and easy since I have a very hectic schedule.
- Scientific proof, testimonies, commonsense information, no gimmicks, something I should be able to follow for the rest of my life, something that combines all food groups and stresses moderation.
- Solid facts with life experiences.
- Persuasion that I need to change.
- I already have the information but not the motivation.
- Strong statistics.
- Alternatives to eating from boredom or emotional reasons.
- My husband and I are in our late fifties and see people on so many drugs and having serious reactions to combinations of drugs. They need to know that pills are not the answer; better eating is. We feel strongly about the Pritikin program.
- I don't need a specific diet telling me what to eat; I need a philosophy that is easily adaptable to a busy lifestyle. I would also like to see biblical connections.
- Self-discipline. You can't address weight and health in your life without addressing Christ in your life.
- How eating poorly is related to stress.
- Statistics enough to scare me.
- Pictures of what foods will do to your arteries.
- It's not the information; it's the motivation.

A lot of these answers surprised me. I thought at this point in our society's understanding of food that most people would be concerned about *how* to eat differently, not *why*. In some ways it was a dramatic eye-opener to see the number of people who said they would need facts or statistics before believing that certain foods were harmful to their health. It makes me glad we provided just that in this book.

QUESTION: *If you have had success at weight loss and have kept it off, what has helped you accomplish this?*

- Exercise, disciplined eating, prayer.
- Eating plenty of low- or nonfat foods.
- Dedication and resolve.
- Exercising and maintaining what I eat.
- Knowing that often my cravings for food really represent unmet needs in my life.
- Not being around food, being preoccupied with other things, and keeping my mind on other projects.
- Eating the right foods and less of them.
- Constant dieting, following an exercise program, and weighing myself the same day each week.
- Keeping track of what I eat, food diary, small-group support, weekly meetings.
- Watching carbohydrate and sugar intake; Eating protein.
- Eating only when I am truly hungry.
- Eliminating all foods that are high in processed sugar.
- Accepting Jesus Christ as my personal Savior opened the door to the self-control I needed to get control of my eating.
- Getting exercise, eating more proteins, cutting out sugars, and limiting carbohydrates.
- Participating in the Zone diet worked very well for me. I had more lean muscle mass, higher energy, and less problems with colds and other nagging illnesses.
- Maintaining the philosophy that if food is in the state that God created it in, then I can eat it. If the food has been made artificially or processed, then I don't eat it.
- Prayers from children.
- Getting exercise, stopping snacking, stopping eating before feeling full.
- I eat everything I want, but some foods only once every six months. I eat nothing in excess and stop eating when I am full.

- Following a modified Atkins diet I dropped twenty-two pounds over a couple of months by cutting sugar, potatoes, bread, and pasta. I ate lean meats, seafood, chicken, low-carbohydrate vegetables and fruits. I snacked on nuts, cheese, and raw carrots.
- Years ago I was in a program called Weight Warriors, which focused on Scripture and healthy eating. I lost thirty pounds and kept it off for five years, until I started dating my husband.
- Being concerned about leaving my family behind just a little too early, mainly due to heart disease.
- The Lord.
- Eating smaller portions at mealtime, no seconds, healthy snacks.
- Walking more, skipping dessert, not eating after dinner.
- A support group.
- Eating to live, not living to eat.
- Exercising, not buying or making breads and desserts.
- Whenever I put God in control, I feel more accountable when I fall off the wagon.
- Combining aerobics and prayer.
- Pushing back from the table.
- Cutting my portions in half, eating when I'm hungry, and stopping when I'm full.

QUESTION: *What do you consider to be healthy foods?*
- Vegetables
- Fruits and juices
- Whole grains
- Lean meats (chicken and fish)
- Milk and dairy, yogurt
- Water
- Cottage cheese
- Seeds
- Green foods

QUESTION: *What do you consider to be unhealthy foods?*
- Deep-fried anything
- Foods high in sugar (candy)
- Cokes and all carbonated drinks

- Fatty meats/red meats
- Skin on chicken
- Donuts
- Cakes

What these results told me was that people have a fairly sophisticated understanding of what to eat. It's the idea of why and how that they get hung up on. Why eat correctly when it's faster, easier, and less expensive to eat foods that contain harmful chemicals, additives, and processing? In a sense the people were saying, "We're happy eating this way. Show us why we shouldn't!"

And of course the biggest issue of all came up again and again. Tell us how we can implement this type of eating in our family and home when we've been eating the other way for years and even decades.

I pray that the answers have been clear in this book. Success in eating can be addressed only by looking at the bigger picture and by incorporating God's grace and power in every aspect of your life. Then you'll understand the amazing connection between food and love and how God's power is the only way to make it all come together.

CHAPTER ONE: A PERSONAL JOURNEY

1. Psalm 50:15, NIV.
2. James 1:17.
3. See Romans 8:28.
4. I surveyed thousands of people who attended my seminars. Some of the results are sprinkled through this book, and others are found in appendix B, "Responses to the Smalley Survey."

CHAPTER TWO: THE AMAZING CONNECTION

1. Kathleen DesMaisons, *Potatoes Not Prozac* (New York: Simon & Schuster, 1999).
2. Dean Ornish, *Love and Survival* (New York: HarperCollins, 1998), 2–3.

CHAPTER FOUR: FOODS THAT THREATEN OUR EMOTIONAL HEALTH

1. Elizabeth Somer, *Food and Mood: The Complete Guide to Eating Well and Feeling Your Best* (New York: Henry Holt, 1999), 5–32.
2. Ibid., 13.
3. Kay Sheppard, *From the First Bite: A Complete Guide to Recovery from Food Addiction* (Deerfield Beach, Fla.: Health Communications, 2000), 47–52.
4. Somer, *Food and Mood*, 112–13.
5. Sheppard, *From the First Bite*, 47–52.
6. Cheryl Townsley, *Food Smart!* (New York: Putnam, 1997), 102.
7. John Yudkin, quoted in Townsley, *Food Smart!*, 102.
8. Nancy Appleton, *Lick the Sugar Habit* (Garden City Park, N.Y.: Avery Publishing Group, 1996), 139–40.
9. William Sears and Martha Sears, *The Family Nutrition Book* (New York: Little, Brown, 1999), 38.
10. Kathleen DesMaisons, *Potatoes Not Prozac* (New York: Smion & Schuster, 1999), 69–70.
11. Townsley, *Food Smart!*, 106.
12. Sheppard, *From the First Bite*, 49–50.
13. Ibid.
14. DesMaisons, *Potatoes Not Prozac*, 43–46.
15. Somer, *Food and Mood*, 27–32.
16. Townsley, *Food Smart!*, 102.

CHAPTER FIVE: FOODS THAT STRENGTHEN OUR EMOTIONAL HEALTH

1. Elizabeth Somer, *Food and Mood: The Complete Guide to Eating Well and Feeling Your Best* (New York: Henry Holt, 1999), 191–214.
2. Rex Russell, *What the Bible Says about Healthy Living* (Glendale, Calif.: Regal, 1996), 29.
3. Proverbs 24:13, NIV; Proverbs 16:24, NLT; Proverbs 25:16, NIV; Proverbs 25:27, NIV.

4. Russell, *What the Bible Says,* 58–59.

5. Somer, *Food and Mood,* 112–13.

6. William Sears, M.D., and Martha Sears, *The Family Nutrition Book* (New York: Little, Brown, 1999), 205–206.

7. Ibid., 211.

8. Somer, *Food and Mood,* 274–75.

9. Ibid., 186.

10. Ibid., 47–53.

11. Leviticus 11 lists "clean" and "unclean" animals.

12. David Macht, "An Experimental Pharmacological Appreciation of Leviticus XI and Deuteronomy XIV," *Bulletin of Historical Medicine* (Johns Hopkins University) 47, no. 1 (April 1953): 444–50.

13. Ibid., 276–79.

14. Adapted from Townsley, *Food Smart!,* 28.

15. Anne Frähm, *Cancer Battle Plan,* quoted in Townsley, *Food Smart!,* 30.

16. I like a Shaklee product, Shaklee Basic H, but other products are available in the produce department of most large grocery stores.

17. Robert Pritikin, *The Pritikin Weight Loss Breakthrough* (New York: Dutton, 1998), 62.

CHAPTER SIX: WHEN FOOD THREATENS OUR EMOTIONAL HEALTH

1. Kathleen DesMaisons, *Potatoes Not Prozac* (New York: Simon & Schuster, 1999), 43.

2. Deirdra Price, *Healing the Hungry Self* (New York: Plume, 1998), 12–14.

3. DesMaisons, *Potatoes Not Prozac,* 42.

4. Ibid., 57–77.

5. Ibid., 41–44.

6. Elizabeth Somer, *Food and Mood* (New York: Holt, 1995), 106–109.

7. Ibid., 13–15.

8. DesMaisons, *Potatoes Not Prozac,* 130.

9. Ibid., 21–22.

10. Ibid., 41–44.

CHAPTER SEVEN:
HOW POOR EMOTIONAL HEALTH CAN AFFECT MARRIAGE

1. Kay Sheppard, *From the First Bite: A Complete Guide to Recovery from Food Addiction* (Deerfield Beach, Fla.: Health Communications, 2000), 47–52.

2. H. Leighton Steward, *Sugar Busters!* (New York: Ballantine Books, 1998).

3. Ibid.

CHAPTER EIGHT: POOR RELATIONSHIPS LEAD TO POOR HEALTH

1. R. M. Nerem, M. J. Levesque, and J. F. Cornhill, "Social Environment as a Factor in Diet-Induced Arteriosclerosis," *Science* 208 (1980): 1475–76.

2. J. H. Medalie et al., "The Importance of Biopsychosocial Factors in the Development of Duodenal Ulcer in a Cohort of Middle-Aged Men," *American Journal of Epidemiology* 136 (1992): 1280–87.

3. Dean Ornish, *Love and Survival* (New York: HarperCollins, 1998), 42.

4. Ibid., 42–43.

5. Ibid., 127–29.

6. S. Cohen et al., "Social Ties and Susceptibility to the Common Cold," *Journal of the American Medical Association* 277 (1997): 1940–44.

7. Ornish, *Love and Survival,* 58–59.

8. Ibid., 24–25.

9. Ibid., 27–28.

10. "Coronary-Prone Behavior and Coronary Heart Disease: A Critical Review," *Circulation* 65 (1978): 1199–1215.

CHAPTER NINE: LOVE AS THE KEY TO HEALTH

1. Dean Ornish, *Love and Survival* (New York: HarperCollins, 1998), 28.

2. Philippians 2:3-5.

3. See Matthew 22:37-39; Mark 12:30-31.

4. Adapted from Ornish, *Love and Survival,* 39–71.

5. Ibid., 42–43.

6. Ibid., 45–46.

7. A. J. Cunningham and C. V. I. Edmonds, "Group Psychological Therapy for Cancer Patients: A Point of View and Discussion of the Hierarchy of Options," *International Journal of Psychiatry in Medicine* 26 (1996): 51–82.

8. K. M. Allen, J. T. Blascovich, and R. M. Kelsey, "Presence of Human Friends and Pet Dogs as Moderators of Autonomic Responses to Stress in Women," *Journal of Personality and Social Psychology* 61 (1991): 582–89.

9. Ornish, *Love and Survival,* 70–71.

10. Matthew 22:37-39.

CHAPTER TEN: EFFECTS OF CONFLICT AND ISOLATION IN MARRIAGE

1. Howard Markman, Scott Stanley, and Susan L. Blumberg, *Fighting for Your Marriage: Positive Steps for Preventing Divorce and Preserving a Lasting Love* (San Francisco: Jossey-Bass, 1994).

2. Matthew 12:20, NIV.

3. Markman, Stanley, and Blumberg, *Fighting for Your Marriage.*

4. Ibid.

5. B. Egolf et al., "Featuring Health Risks and Mortality: The Roseto Effect: A 50-Year Comparison of Mortality Rates," *American Journal of Public Health* 82 (1992): 1089–92.

6. Ibid.

7. Gary Oliver and Norm Wright have written several books about how to handle anger effectively. I recommend Gary J. Oliver and H. Norman Wright, *When Anger Hits Home: Taking Care of Your Anger without Taking It Out on Your Family* (Chicago: Moody Press, 1992) and Gary J. Oliver and H. Norman Wright, *Good Women Get Angry: A Woman's Guide to Handling Her Anger, Depression, Anxiety, and Stress* (Ann Arbor, Mich.: Servant, 1995).

8. J. C. Barefoot et al., "Suspiciousness, Health, and Mortality: A Follow-Up Study of 500 Older Adults," *Psychosomatic Medicine* 49 (1987): 450–57.

9. R. B. Shekelle, W. J. Raynor, and A. M. Ostfeld, "Personality and Risk of Cancer: 20-Year Follow-Up of the Western Electric Study," *Psychosomatic Medicine* 43 (1981): 117–25.

10. G. A. Kaplan et al., "Social Connections and Mortality from All Causes and from Cardiovascular Disease: Prospective Evidence from Eastern Finland," *American Journal of Epidemiology* 128 (1988): 370–80.

11. Visit the Smalley Relationship Center Web site—Smalleyonline.com—to find a small group in your area. PRISM weight-loss program is famous for their small-group approach; see Karen Kingsbury with Toni Vogt, *The PRISM Weight Loss Program* (Sisters, Ore.: Multnomah, 1999).

CHAPTER ELEVEN:
L-O-V-E: THE CURE FOR CONFLICT AND ISOLATION

1. James 1:19.

2. John M. Gottman and Nan Silver, *The Seven Principles for Making Marriage Work* (New York: Crown Publishers, 1999).

3. Romans 12:10, NIV.

4. Psalm 103:1, NASB.

CHAPTER TWELVE: CHEAP SUBSTITUTES FOR LOVE

1. Gregory L. Jantz, *Hope, Help, and Healing for Eating Disorders: A New Approach to Treating Anorexia, Bulimia, and Overeating* (Wheaton, Ill.: Harold Shaw, 1995), 23.

2. Ibid.

3. Ibid.

4. Dean Ornish, *Love and Survival* (New York: HarperCollins, 1998), 57–58.

CHAPTER THIRTEEN: TEN WAYS TO EXTEND GRACE WHEN WEIGHT IS AN ISSUE FOR YOU OR YOUR SPOUSE

1. Luke 1:37.

2. Gerald G. May, *Addiction and Grace* (New York: HarperCollins, 1991).

3. James 1:2.

CHAPTER FOURTEEN: IF NOTHING ELSE HAS WORKED

1. Karen Kingsbury and Toni Vogt, *The PRISM Weight Loss Program* (Sisters, Ore.: Multnomah, 1999), 37–75.

2. Romans 7:8.

3. Hebrews 10:1.

4. Romans 7, *The Message*, emphasis in the original.

5. Zechariah 4:6, NIV; Philippians 4:13; Acts 1:8, NIV; Galatians 5:16-18; Galatians 5:22-23, emphasis added; 1 John 5:3-4; Romans 10:4.

6. Romans 7, *The Message*.

7. Romans 8, *The Message*.

CHAPTER FIFTEEN: SEVEN STEPS TO LIFELONG VICTORY

1. 1 Peter 5:7.

2. Gerald G. May, *Addiction and Grace* (New York: HarperCollins, 1988), 38-39.
3. James 4:6-8, NIV.
4. 2 Corinthians 7:10.
5. James 4:10.
6. Genesis 1:26; 1 Corinthians 1:2; Ephesians 2:10; Romans 5:17; Ephesians 1:6.
7. Psalm 50:15, NIV.
8. Ephesians 2:4-5, NIV.
9. Ephesians 6:10-14.
10. Psalm 130:5-6, NIV.
11. See 2 Peter 3:8.
12. See Luke 18:1-5.
13. Isaiah 40:31.
14. Ephesians 3:20-21, NIV.
15. 2 Corinthians 12:9-10, NIV.
16. James 1:2-4.
17. Luke 11:10.
18. See Luke 11:11-13.
19. Mark 11:25.
20. See Malachi 2:13-16.
21. Hebrews 11:1.
22. Mark 11:23-24.
23. Luke 18:1-8.
24. Luke 18:7-8, NIV.
25. Paraphrase of Luke 11:5-8.
26. Luke 11:9-10.

CHAPTER SIXTEEN: THE AMAZING CONNECTION

1. Isaiah 61:3.
2. Ecclesiastes 3:11, NIV.
3. Romans 8:1-2.
4. Ephesians 3:16-21.

CHAPER SEVENTEEN: SPECIAL CONCERNS FOR THE SINGLE PERSON

1. See Hebrews 13:5.
2. Hebrews 13:8.
3. See James 4:8.

CHAPTER EIGHTEEN: FREQUENTLY ASKED QUESTIONS

1. Calvin Ezrin, with Kristen L. Caron, *Your Fat Can Make You Thin* (Los Angeles: Lowell House, 2000), 17–28.
2. Karen Kingsbury and Toni Vogt, *The PRISM Weight Loss Program* (Sisters, Ore.: Multnomah, 1999), 153–166.
3. Michael Wargovich, quoted in Rex Russell, *What the Bible Says about Healthy Living* (Glendale, Calif.: Regal, 1996), 49, 53.

D R. GARY SMALLEY, founder and chairman of the board of the Smalley Relationship Center, is one of the country's best-known authors and speakers on family relationships. He is the author and coauthor of eighteen books, including the best-selling, award-winning books *Marriage for a Lifetime, Secrets to Lasting Love, The Blessing* (with John Trent), *The Two Sides of Love* (with John Trent), and *The Language of Love* (with John Trent), as well as *Bound by Honor* (with his son Greg Smalley). Gary has also produced several popular films and videos.

In his thirty years of ministry Gary has spoken to more than two million people in conferences. He has been presenting his two-day workshop "Love Is a Decision" once a month for more than twenty years. His award-winning infomercial "Hidden Keys to Loving Relationships" has been viewed by television audiences all over the world. Several versions of the infomercial—first with Dick Clark, then with John Tesh and Connie Selleca, and also with Frank and Kathie Lee Gifford—have been aired.

Gary has appeared on national television programs such as *Oprah, Larry King Live, Today Show, Sally Jessy Raphael,* as well as numerous national radio programs. Gary has been featured on hundreds of regional and local television and radio programs across the United States.

Gary has earned an M.Div. from Bethel Seminary and a doctorate from Biola University. Southwest Baptist University (Missouri) gave him an honorary doctorate for his work with couples.

Gary is partnering with his three grown children in ministry to married couples and families. Dr. Greg Smalley founded a full-service counseling center in Branson, Missouri. Michael Smalley is a marriage therapist with a masters degree from Wheaton College Graduate School. Kari Smalley Gibson is a successful author of children's books. Gary and his wife, Norma, have been married for nearly forty years and live in Branson, Missouri. They have been blessed with seven grandchildren.

To find out more about the resources of the Smalley Relationship Center or to schedule speaking engagements, use these contact numbers:

The Smalley Relationship Center
1482 Lakeshore Drive
Branson, MO 65616
PHONE: (417) 335-4321 • FAX: (417) 336-3515
WEB SITE: www.smalleyonline.com